GREAT PARTIES

GREAT PARTIES

Recipes, Menus, and Ideas for Perfect Gatherings

The Best of Martha Stewart Living

Thanks to the many hosts, food editors, stylists, art directors,
photographers, writers, and editors whose inspirational ideas and recipes make up this volume.
And gratitude to the entire staff of Martha Stewart Living Omnimedia and to everyone
at Oxmoor House, Clarkson Potter, Satellite Graphics, and Quebecor Printing
whose invaluable work helped produce this book.

Manufactured in the United States of America.
Library of Congress Catalog Number: 97-66606
ISBN 0-8487-1629-9 (hardcover)
0-8487-1657-4 (paperback)

Editor: Bruce Shostak
Designer: Linda Kocur
Writer: Elaine Louie
Managing Editor: Kyle T. Blood
Endpaper design: Eve Ashcraft

CONTENTS

INTRODUCTION

I wrote my very first book in 1982. Titled *Entertaining*, it expressed, as well as I could then, my very intense thoughts about planning and preparing and giving parties of all types—large or small, lavish or simple. I am pleased to say that over the years my philosophy and sentiments have remained the same, and this book, a compilation of the many wonderful entertaining stories and ideas that we, at *Martha Stewart Living*, have worked on with our friends, reveals an identical sensibility. I hope that *Great Parties* shows, as *Entertaining* did, "that there are many ways of entertaining and that each ultimately depends not on pomp or show or elaborate technique, but on thought, effort, and caring—much like friendship itself."

I would personally like to thank all of the people who contributed to this book. We are so fortunate to have such loyal and interested friends across the country. They opened up their particular worlds to us and let us not only peek into but also enter their homes and kitchens and backyards. We cooked with them, met their friends, and drank their wines, and had a fabulous time learning their personal secrets about hosting large crowds as well as intimate gatherings.

The recipes throughout *Great Parties* reflect our beliefs about freshness and goodness, but they don't ignore the fact that great party food must be plentiful, beautiful, and delicious. Entertaining is and always will be about caring—caring about people, originality, the most attractive settings, and lovely, finely honed, time-honored traditions.

Martha Stewart

LOUISIANA
OUTDOOR LUNCH

CHILLED BLOODY-MARY SOUP WITH CRABMEAT

BENNE-SEED WAFERS

MAQUECHOUX OYSTERS
WITH RED-PEPPER MAYONNAISE

SWEET-POTATO BISCUITS

PECAN-CRUSTED CATFISH WITH WILTED GREENS
AND TOMATO CHUTNEY

RED-BEAN-AND-RICE SALAD

BANANA-BOURBON LAYER CAKE

OPPOSITE: At the Parlange home in Louisiana, fragrant magnolia blossoms in jars and vases await placement on the lunch table; nineteenth-century glass fly catchers filled with sugared water attract flies away from food.

On a hot day, with the humidity palpable, eating outdoors is a wonderfully sensual experience—as long as there is shade.

In the Deep South, where summer arrives early and lingers, residents have perfected the art of hot-weather dining in the out-of-doors. Especially when the heat and the humidity top ninety, as is often the case, shade of every sort is the ally, allowing diners to enjoy the calls of doves and the sweet smell of magnolia. At Parlange, Walter Parlange, Jr., (whose forebears built the rural French-colonial house) and his wife, Lucy, take cocktails with guests in the cool, gray-green shadows of cypress and live oaks laced with Spanish moss. Classic mint juleps are served in silver tumblers, the frosty beads of sweat promising cool comfort. In due time, lunch is taken on the gallery—screened porches or umbrella-shaded tables will suffice in other locales. The meal is meant to be slow, languorous, soothing, and everything is aimed at achieving that end. The table is set with white linens, heirloom china, and sterling silver; comfortable chairs are brought from the dining room. The dishes are chosen from a time-honored Southern repertoire—cornmeal-fried oysters, bitter mustard greens, sweet-potato biscuits. Chilled white wine is poured into crystal goblets. The food and libations are arrayed on the wide banister, a gracious invitation for people to stroll. If a silver tumbler tumbles off the rail, Miss Lucy shrugs: "What's a few dents between friends?"

TOP, LEFT TO RIGHT: A welcome from Miss Lucy Parlange, the hostess. "Calling Card" cotton organdy fabric designed by Angèle Parlange, Miss Lucy's daughter, covers the chair seats and adds a note of whimsy to the cool, elegant table setting. Walter Parlange, Jr., in the fedora, Angèle to his left, begins lunch with his guests at his home, Parlange, on the False River, outside Baton Rouge, Louisiana. ABOVE LEFT: Antique calling cards from the Paris salon of her great-grandmother were the inspiration for Angèle's fabric. OPPOSITE: Ready for mint juleps, a tray of silver cups gleams on the gallery.

An island of crabmeat rises out of the chilled tomato soup, a cross between gazpacho and a Bloody Mary; benne-seed wafers, made with sesame seeds, are set around the table to accompany the soup.

Chilled Bloody-Mary Soup With Crabmeat

serves 8 to 10

A cold soup is always a refreshing first course on a hot day; this one doesn't require any time on the stove at all.

6 *ripe tomatoes*
4 *large red bell peppers, seeded*
2 *large green bell peppers, seeded*
2 *cucumbers, peeled and seeded*
3 *stalks celery, strings removed*
1 *small clove garlic*
1 *red onion*
3 *tablespoons olive oil*
   Juice of 2 limes, or to taste
4 *tablespoons Worcestershire sauce*
   Salt and freshly ground pepper
   Tabasco, to taste
2 *tablespoons freshly grated or prepared horseradish, or to taste*
½ *cup vodka, optional*
1 *pound jumbo lump crabmeat, picked over for shells and cartilage*

1. Cut the vegetables, garlic, and onion into large chunks, and purée in batches in a blender or food processor, adding some of the olive oil to each batch.
2. Strain through a sieve into a large bowl to remove skins and seeds.
3. Add lime juice, Worcestershire sauce, salt and pepper to taste, Tabasco, horseradish, and vodka, if desired. Cover; chill for at least 2 hours, or overnight. Taste before serving; adjust seasonings if necessary. The amount of lime juice needed will depend on the acidity of tomatoes.
4. Ladle into soup bowls; place ¼ cup of crabmeat in the center of each. Grate additional fresh horseradish over surface of soup, if desired. Serve immediately.

Benne-Seed Wafers

makes 32

Nutty, slightly sweet sesame seeds, called benne seeds in the South, were brought to America from Africa.

2 *large eggs*
1 *tablespoon olive oil*
1 *cup plus 1 tablespoon all-purpose flour*
¼ *teaspoon salt*
½ *teaspoon baking powder*
   Large pinch of sugar
¾ *cup unhulled sesame seeds, toasted*
1 *egg mixed with 1 tablespoon water, for egg wash*

1. Heat oven to 350°. In medium bowl, beat together eggs and oil until frothy. In another bowl, combine flour, salt, baking powder, sugar, and sesame seeds. Mix into egg mixture. Add extra flour if needed to make a stiff, but not sticky, dough.
2. Roll out dough on a lightly floured board as thinly as possible. Using a 3-inch-round biscuit cutter, cut dough into circles. Arrange on a greased or parchment-lined baking sheet. Brush lightly with egg wash. Poke holes all over crackers with a fork, making sure that the holes go all the way through.
3. Bake for 10 minutes, or until brown around edges. Turn over, and bake 4 minutes more, or until golden brown and crisp. Let cool; store in airtight container.

good thing

Mint Juleps The mint julep is emblematic of the South. Originating in either Maryland or Virginia, it had as its main ingredient brandy, rum, or rye, but when the mint julep reached Kentucky, bourbon became the liquor of choice. The julep is a drink that provokes cheerful debate. Martha likes to bruise the mint leaves, to release the aromatic oils. Others, who don't care for the slight tinge of bitterness, prefer their mint sprigs untouched. Whatever your method, either shave or crush the ice, so that the drink is quickly chilled and diluted. As for the sugar, make a syrup of sugar boiled with water that blends smoothly with the liquor. Silver cups are preferred since they frost better than glass. For a nonedible nontoxic garnish, you can tuck a camellia, verbena, or camomile into each drink.

ABOVE: Cornmeal-fried oysters are served with a red-pepper mayonnaise and a spicy maquechoux, a traditional Cajun dish that is made in as many ways as there are cooks; the only constant is corn.

Maquechoux Oysters

serves 8

3½ dozen oysters, in the shells

4 ears fresh yellow corn, husked

1 tablespoon olive oil

1 large onion, peeled and finely diced

½ teaspoon salt
  Dash of cayenne pepper

1 large red bell pepper, cut into ¼-inch dice

2 jalapeño peppers
  Oil, for frying

2 cups yellow cornmeal
  Red-Pepper Mayonnaise (recipe follows)

1. Scrub oysters well with a brush under running water. Discard any that are open or have broken shells. Shuck oysters, saving all liquid and bottom halves of shells. Scrub shells inside and out; set aside. Refrigerate oysters in reserved liquid, covered, until ready to use.

2. Cut corn from cobs; set aside. Heat oil in a medium sauté pan over medium-low heat. Add onion, and cook, covered, until translucent, about 10 minutes.

3. Add corn, and cook, stirring, for about 5 minutes, or until corn is softened. Add salt, cayenne, red pepper, and jalapeños, and cook for 2 minutes.

4. Drain the oysters, reserving liquid. Measure liquid, and add enough water to make 1 cup. Pour into pan. Turn heat up to medium; cook about 10 minutes, or until liquid is mostly reduced. Set aside.

5. In a large skillet, heat about 1 inch of oil to 375°. Dredge the oysters in the cornmeal, coating them entirely. Fry them in batches (they shouldn't overlap), and drain on paper towels.

6. Arrange 4 or 5 oyster shells on each plate. Spoon about 1 teaspoon of Red-Pepper Mayonnaise into each shell, and top with an oyster and some of the corn mixture. Serve immediately.

Red-Pepper Mayonnaise

makes 1 cup

1 large red bell pepper

1 large egg yolk (see Note)

1 teaspoon salt

¼ teaspoon cayenne pepper

1 large clove garlic, or to taste
  Juice of 1 lemon

¾ cup olive oil

1. Roast pepper over a gas flame or under broiler until skin is completely blackened. Place in a paper bag until cool. Peel and seed pepper.

2. Place pepper in a blender or mini food processor with all ingredients except oil. Blend until smooth. With motor running, begin adding oil a few drops at a time. As mixture starts to thicken, pour in remaining oil in a slow, steady stream, and mix until incorporated. Cover, and refrigerate for up to 3 days.

Note: Raw eggs should not be used in food prepared for pregnant women, babies, young children, the elderly, or anyone whose health is compromised.

Sweet-Potato Biscuits

makes 12

These spicy biscuits taste especially good warm from the oven, but are also wonderful served at room temperature.

1   *pound (about 4) sweet potatoes*
2½   *cups all-purpose flour*
4   *teaspoons baking powder*
2   *tablespoons sugar*
1   *teaspoon salt*
¼   *teaspoon cayenne pepper*
8   *tablespoons (1 stick) unsalted butter, chilled*
¼   *cup milk*

1. Heat oven to 400°. Wash the sweet potatoes, and prick all over with a fork. Place on a baking sheet; bake until soft, about 1 hour. (The juices will start to run out.) When cool enough to handle, scoop out flesh and press through a sieve (you should have 1¼ cups of purée). Set aside.
2. In a mixing bowl, combine the dry ingredients. Cut in butter until mixture resembles coarse meal.
3. In another bowl, whisk together milk and sweet-potato purée. Add to dry ingredients, and mix until well combined.
4. Place dough on lightly floured board, knead once or twice, and pat out to ½ inch thick. Cut out biscuits with a floured 2-inch-round cutter. Bake on parchment-lined baking sheet for about 20 minutes, or until golden brown.

ABOVE: Sweet-potato biscuits, piled on Miss Lucy's ironstone pedestal stand, make a colorful and appetizing pyramid.

ABOVE: A white linen tablecloth and old Paris-porcelain china make simple backdrops for pecan-crusted catfish, mustard greens, red-bean-and-rice salad, and sweet-potato biscuits; although by no means Spartan, the meal represents enlightened regional cooking—fish baked not fried, greens lightly braised.

Pecan-Crusted Catfish With Wilted Greens and Tomato Chutney

serves 8

To make coating fish neater and easier, use one hand for flouring and coating with nuts, and the other for dipping in egg.

  4   cups pecans
  ½ cup all-purpose flour
     Salt and freshly ground pepper
     Cayenne pepper
  1   large egg
  3   tablespoons milk
  8   catfish or red-snapper fillets, about 4
     ounces each
  2   bunches (about 1½ pounds) mustard
     greens or kale
     Juice of 1 lemon
     Tomato Chutney (recipe follows)

1. Heat oven to 450°. Grind pecans in a food processor with on-off pulses, leaving some larger pieces intact and some of the pecans almost a powder. Spread on a plate, and set aside.
2. Mix flour with salt, pepper, and cayenne to taste. Spread out on a plate. Whisk together egg and milk in a shallow bowl.
3. Rinse fish, and pat dry. Coat with seasoned flour, shaking off excess. Dip in egg mixture, letting excess drip off. Firmly press on pecans, coating fish completely.
4. Arrange fillets on a baking sheet, being careful not to overlap. Place in oven, and bake for 15 minutes.
5. While fish is baking, wash the greens, allowing a little moisture to cling to the leaves. Tear into medium-size pieces, and place in a large pot. Sprinkle with salt. Cover, and cook over medium heat, stirring occasionally, for 3 to 5 minutes, or until the greens are wilted and bright green. Season greens to taste with lemon juice and pepper.
6. Place a serving of greens on each of 8 plates, and lay a fish fillet on top. Spoon a few tablespoons of the chutney on each fillet, and serve immediately.

Tomato Chutney

makes 1 cup

This simple sweet-and-sour condiment goes well with fish or chicken.

  4   plum tomatoes
  4   shallots
  1   cup water
  4   tablespoons sugar
  4   tablespoons balsamic vinegar
  3   drops Tabasco, or to taste

1. Cut a small "x" in the bottom of each tomato. Bring a pot of water to a boil, lower tomatoes into it, and return to a boil. Count to 10, and lift out tomatoes with a slotted spoon; then plunge them into ice water. Peel tomatoes, and cut off flesh in large pieces. Discard cores or save for another use. Cut tomatoes into long strips about ¼ inch wide. Place strips in a colander over a bowl; allow to drain.
2. Peel shallots and slice them crosswise about ⅛ inch thick. Place in a shallow skillet along with the water and sugar. Cook over medium heat, swirling pan occasionally, until liquid is reduced to a thick, clear syrup, 15 to 20 minutes.
3. Add vinegar, tomatoes, and Tabasco, and cook for 5 minutes, gently stirring. The chutney should be thick, but the tomatoes shouldn't break down very much. Let cool. Serve chutney cold or at room temperature.

don't forget

• As the sun shifts, shade may vanish. Be sure the site of the meal will remain shaded during the hours you plan to entertain.

• Pale settings and decorations look cool. Set the table with a white tablecloth, white linen damask napkins, and creamy magnolias, a soothing oasis even when the humidity is high.

• Provide a straw or folding paper fan at each place setting so your guests can cool themselves in case the air is still. The visual effect is soothing, too.

• In hot, humid weather, cook as many dishes as possible the day before. Start the meal with a chilled soup, and avoid serving too many warm entrées.

• Along with mint juleps and chilled white wine, have cold nonalcoholic drinks available, like lemonade, iced tea, and water.

• Chairs on the lawn and hammocks strung between trees are natural invitations to a post-lunch siesta. At the end of a large meal, a Southern custom is to exclaim, "I'm full as a tick."

Red-Bean-and-Rice Salad

serves 8 to 10

Louisiana popcorn and Indian basmati rices are both long-grain varieties of aromatic rice with subtle, nutty flavors.

- ¼ cup red kidney beans
- 1 bay leaf
- 1 teaspoon salt, plus more to taste
- 2 cups long-grain rice, preferably basmati or popcorn rice
- 1 cucumber, peeled and seeded
- 2 stalks celery, peeled to remove strings
- 4 scallions, white and green parts, sliced into small rounds
- Spicy Vinaigrette (recipe follows)

1. Pick over beans; discard any broken ones and foreign objects. Rinse and place in a large saucepan. Add bay leaf and water to cover by 2 inches. Bring water to a boil. Turn down heat, and cook at a steady simmer for 1 to 1½ hours. Cooking time will vary according to the age of the beans. Toward the end of the cooking time, add salt to taste. Let cool in liquid; drain when cool, and discard bay leaf.
2. Place rice in a 2-quart saucepan with a tight-fitting lid. Add 3½ cups water and 1 teaspoon salt. Bring to a boil. Turn down to a simmer, cover, and cook for 20 minutes. Remove from heat, and let stand, covered, for 10 minutes. Fluff with a fork, and transfer to a bowl.
3. Cut cucumber and celery into ¼-inch dice. Add to rice along with beans and scallions. Toss with vinaigrette. Serve at room temperature within a few hours.

Spicy Vinaigrette

makes 1 cup

- 3 tablespoons fresh thyme leaves, or 1 tablespoon dried
- ¾ cup olive oil
- 4 tablespoons red-wine vinegar
- 2 tablespoons freshly squeezed lemon juice
- ⅛ teaspoon cayenne pepper
- ½ teaspoon salt
- 1 clove garlic, peeled and slightly crushed
- ¾ teaspoon freshly ground pepper

Chop thyme leaves to release the flavor. In a small bowl, combine remaining ingredients. Add chopped thyme; whisk well. Remove garlic clove before serving.

Banana-Bourbon Layer Cake

serves 8 to 10

Prepare the sliced-banana topping just before serving.

For the cake:
- 2¼ cups all-purpose flour
- ¾ teaspoon baking soda
- ½ teaspoon baking powder
- ½ teaspoon salt
- 8 tablespoons (1 stick) unsalted butter, at room temperature
- 1½ cups granulated sugar
- 3 large eggs, separated
- 2 to 3 ripe bananas, enough to make 1 cup mashed
- ½ cup buttermilk
- 1 teaspoon pure vanilla extract

For the filling:
- 1 cup heavy cream
- 2 tablespoons confectioners' sugar
- ¾ cup sour cream

For the topping:
- 3 bananas, not too ripe
- 2 tablespoons unsalted butter
- 2 tablespoons dark-brown sugar
- ¾ cup bourbon

1. Heat oven to 350°. Grease and flour two 8-inch-round cake pans. In a bowl, sift together flour, baking soda, baking powder, and salt. Set aside.
2. Cream together butter and granulated sugar. Add egg yolks one at a time. In another bowl, mash bananas; combine with buttermilk and vanilla. Add alternately to the butter mixture with the flour mixture, beginning and ending with flour.
3. Beat egg whites until they are stiff; fold into batter.
4. Divide batter between prepared pans. Bake 30 to 35 minutes, or until a toothpick inserted into center comes out clean. Let cool in pans for 5 minutes, then turn out onto a rack to cool completely.
5. When cake layers are cool, whip cream with confectioners' sugar until stiff. Fold in sour cream. Place a cake layer on a plate, and spread with filling to within 1 inch of edge. Place other layer on top, and press down lightly. Chill for 1 hour.
6. Slice bananas ½ inch thick. Melt the butter in a large sauté pan over medium heat. When it sizzles, add the slices in a single layer. Sprinkle with dark-brown sugar. When golden brown, turn slices; cook until brown on other side.
7. Pour in bourbon (use a measuring cup; never pour straight from the bottle), and carefully ignite with a match. Cook until the flames die down, shaking the pan to toss bananas in syrup. Remove from heat.
8. Arrange banana slices on top of cake. Pour remaining syrup over cake, letting it drip down sides. Serve immediately.

ABOVE: The unhurried lunch ends with a glazed, two-layer banana-bourbon cake, an irresistible variation on the classic New Orleans dessert Bananas Foster.

MEDITERRANEAN BUFFET

ITALIAN SODAS

PEPERONATA

CHICKPEA SALSA

STUFFED GRAPE LEAVES

TOMATILLO-AVOCADO SALSA

WILD-MUSHROOM CROSTINI

BABA GHANOUSH

FIG-AND-PROSCIUTTO SANDWICHES

MOCK SPIT-ROASTED CHICKEN

ROAST LEG OF LAMB

HONEYED ONIONS WITH CURRANTS

GRILLED VEGETABLES

ROASTED-CORN SALSA

ICE-CREAM SANDWICHES

OPPOSITE: Summer dusk in the Napa Valley creates an intimate mood, drawing people together and propelling an informal gathering into a feast; a farmhouse table half draped with a white cloth adds to the carefree nature of the event.

At a relaxed and abundant Mediterranean buffet, Napa–style, there's always another place (or two, or three) at the table.

An old friend may be in town. The butcher might call to say he has a spectacular leg of lamb. "Anything can become an event," says Pam Hunter, who, with Carl Doumani, loves to throw drop-of-a-hat evening parties at their winery in Napa Valley, California. Whatever the occasion, an excess of food and wine is always called for, and Pam and Carl always make certain that their outdoor buffets are casual events. Some of the invited guests bring only good conversation. Others ask if they can bring houseguests and the family dog. With their generous spirit, Carl and Pam always say yes, bring everybody, including the dog. Simplicity, from food to flower arrangements to table settings, is what makes the party-giving fun. This menu includes a variety of easy-to-cook foods that can be prepared the night before or the morning of the party. These dishes taste best at room temperature, and mix and match well, like spit-roasted chicken, baba ghanoush, and peperonata. Nearly all can be eaten with fingers, including slices of grilled leg of lamb, which can be tucked into soft breads like pita or tortillas, and eaten with abandon. What unites the meal is the variety of Mediterranean flavors—extra-virgin olive oil, lemon juice, garlic, parsley, and thyme. Some guests will eat just two of their favorites; others will sample a half-dozen dishes. "There's no agenda," says Carl. "If you want things to be perfect, you worry. It's about breaking bread." And, of course, it's also about opening wine.

TOP, LEFT TO RIGHT: A straw-filled basket becomes a nest for bottles of red wine. A loose bouquet of freshly cut roses looks rustic in a French terra-cotta pot. Host Carl Doumani and his son, Jared, spit-roast chickens, turning them every fifteen minutes; the technique can be mimicked in an ordinary oven or over a grill. ABOVE LEFT: Just minutes before preparing the feast, host Pam Hunter gathers vegetables from the garden located next to her kitchen.

TOP LEFT: Riotous clusters of roses, irises, mint, and borage in galvanized-steel buckets are placed on the buffet table, on the porch, and around the premises; the bouquets provide multicolored focal points in an already splendid setting. TOP RIGHT: A parade of choices—(from rear) baba ghanoush, peperonata, tomatillo-avocado salsa, honeyed onions with currants, and roasted-corn salsa—can all be eaten with meat, vegetables, or bread. LEFT: Salad plates are well suited to outdoor meals; guests tend to take smaller servings and return to the buffet when ready for more. Mexican glass gives a watery flicker to ordinary votives; placed inside lanterns, candles won't blow out in the wind.

Italian Sodas

makes one soda

Fruit-, nut-, and herb-flavored syrups are available at specialty-food stores.

1 part flavored syrup, such as Torani
4 parts seltzer or mineral water
Fresh mint or fruit for garnish

Fill a tall glass with ice, add syrup, and fill with seltzer. Stir well. Add more syrup to taste. Garnish with fresh mint or fruit.

Peperonata

makes 1 cup

Serve this colorful Italian condiment with lamb, or use it as a topping for crostini.

3 large bell peppers, preferably 1 each red,
  yellow, and orange
1 large Spanish onion, peeled
1 tablespoon olive oil
1 tablespoon unsalted butter
1 clove garlic, peeled and thinly sliced
  Pinch of sugar
  Salt and freshly ground pepper

1. Stem, seed, and remove ribs from the peppers. Cut lengthwise into 1-inch-wide strips; leave curved ends intact. Cut onion in half lengthwise, and slice into ¼-inch-thick semicircles.

2. Heat oil and butter in a large skillet over medium heat. Add garlic and onions, and cook for about 2 minutes. Add the pepper strips and sugar, and toss for 2 to 3 minutes. Cover pan; turn heat to low. Cook, stirring occasionally, until peppers are very soft, 30 to 35 minutes.

3. Remove cover; raise heat to medium. Cook, stirring often, until most of the liquid evaporates and peppers are nicely glazed, about 3 minutes. Add a little water, if necessary, to avoid scorching. Season with salt and pepper. Serve the peperonata warm or at room temperature.

ABOVE: Flavors of Italy, Greece, and Morocco mix well on a single plate: peperonata, grape leaves stuffed with goat cheese and couscous, and chickpea salsa. RIGHT: Sweet Italian syrups mixed with sparkling water combine to create vivid, flavorful nonalcoholic drinks; tall, clear glasses show off their subtle colors.

Chickpea Salsa

makes 3 cups

To shorten the preparation time, you can substitute canned chickpeas for dried, and start at step 2.

- ½ pound (about 1¼ cups) dried chickpeas, or 2½ cups canned
- 2¼ teaspoons salt, plus more to taste
- ¼ teaspoon cumin seeds or ½ teaspoon ground cumin
- 1 clove garlic, peeled
- 2 teaspoons extra-virgin olive oil
- 4 small dried chiles, stemmed and finely chopped, or ¾ teaspoon red-pepper flakes
- ½ cup oil-cured olives, pitted and coarsely chopped
- 1 tablespoon freshly squeezed lemon juice Freshly ground pepper
- 1 small bunch arugula

1. Pick over dried chickpeas. Rinse and soak overnight in cold water with 1 teaspoon salt. Drain and rinse. Place chickpeas in a medium saucepan, and cover with several inches of fresh water. Bring to a boil, and skim off any foam. Turn heat down to medium, and simmer until tender, 35 to 45 minutes. Ten minutes before chickpeas are done, add ¾ teaspoon salt. Remove from heat; let cool in cooking liquid for about 1 hour.
2. If using cumin seeds, toast in dry pan over medium-low heat until aroma is released, about 2 minutes. Let cool; crush to a powder in a spice grinder. Set aside.
3. Chop together ½ teaspoon salt, garlic, and ½ teaspoon olive oil to form a paste. Add chiles; chop to combine. Transfer to a small bowl, and add remaining oil.
4. Drain soaked chickpeas. (If using canned chickpeas, rinse.) Combine with 1 teaspoon chile mixture, or to taste. Add olives, cumin, lemon juice, and salt and pepper to taste. Refrigerate until ready to serve. Salsa can be made one day ahead; return to room temperature before serving.
5. Just before serving, coarsely chop arugula, and toss with salsa. Serve as a condiment with lamb or chicken.

Grape Leaves Stuffed With Goat Cheese and Couscous

makes about 30

Grape leaves in brine can typically be found in the international-foods section of many supermarkets.

- 1 nine-ounce jar of grape leaves
- ⅓ cup dry couscous
- 1 teaspoon ground cumin Salt and freshly ground pepper
- 1 small tomato, seeded and cut into small dice
- 2 tablespoons finely chopped parsley
- 1 tablespoon olive oil, plus more for sealing and grilling stuffed grape leaves
- 1 tablespoon freshly squeezed lemon juice
- 2 seven-ounce logs goat cheese, cut into ¼-inch disks

1. Rinse and separate grape leaves. Place in a large roasting pan, and cover with boiling water. Let sit until water has cooled somewhat. Rinse in cold water; drain. Pat each leaf dry, clip off stem, and layer between paper towels. Set aside.
2. In a small saucepan, combine couscous, ⅓ cup boiling water, and cumin. Season with salt and pepper. Cover and let stand until couscous is soft and fluffy when stirred with a fork, about 5 minutes.
3. Transfer couscous to a medium bowl, and add tomato, parsley, 1 tablespoon oil, and lemon juice. Toss together, and add salt and pepper; the couscous should be slightly overseasoned.
4. Lay out ten grape leaves at a time on a clean work surface. Place a goat-cheese disk 1 inch from each stem end. Mound a heaping teaspoon of couscous over goat cheese. Fold stem end over filling, then fold sides of leaf over. Dab edges with olive oil to help seal. Fold top of leaf over folded sides, and dab with oil again. Place on a plate, folded-side down, layered between waxed paper. (Stuffed leaves can be prepared up to this point in advance and stored, refrigerated, overnight.)
5. Heat grill or nonstick pan. Brush stuffed leaves with olive oil; place on grill or pan smooth-side down. Grill or sauté until browned, about 2 minutes. Turn carefully, and continue cooking until cheese is soft and filling is heated through, about 2 minutes more. Serve immediately.

Tomatillo-Avocado Salsa

makes 4½ cups

Tomatillos look like small green tomatoes with papery husks. They can be found in Latin-American grocery stores and sometimes in supermarkets.

- 8 ripe tomatillos, husks removed, washed and quartered
- 2 tablespoons freshly squeezed lime juice, plus more to taste
- 3 ripe Hass avocados
- 6 scallions, thinly sliced
- 1 fresh poblano pepper, cut into ¼-inch dice
- ½ small jalapeño pepper, finely minced
- 1 small clove garlic, peeled and finely chopped
- ½ cup cilantro leaves, coarsely chopped Salt and freshly ground pepper

1. Place tomatillos and 2 tablespoons lime juice in a blender or in the bowl of a food processor. Purée until smooth, then transfer mixture to a medium bowl.
2. Cut each avocado lengthwise around pit, and twist halves apart; remove pit. Peel each avocado half, and cut into small dice. Add to tomatillo mixture along with scallions, poblano, jalapeño, garlic, and cilantro. Mix well; season to taste with salt, pepper, and lime juice. Let sit, covered, for 1 hour at room temperature before serving. Serve with grilled meat, fish, or corn tortilla chips.

ABOVE: Sautéed wild mushrooms are served with crostini, grilled slices of bread brushed with olive oil; crostini can be topped with peperonata, baba ghanoush, or any other condiment at the buffet.

Wild-Mushroom Crostini

serves 15

White button mushrooms can be substituted for the wild mushrooms.

1 ounce dried porcini mushrooms
3 cloves garlic, peeled
½ cup flat-leaf parsley, chopped
½ teaspoon kosher salt
1 long loaf of Italian or French bread, sliced ¼ inch thick on the diagonal
   Extra-virgin olive oil, for bread
   Salt and freshly ground pepper
3 tablespoons unsalted butter, or as needed
3 tablespoons olive oil, or as needed
2 shallots, peeled and finely chopped
½ tablespoon fresh thyme leaves, about five sprigs
½ cup dry white wine
2 pounds assorted wild mushrooms, such as shiitake, cremini, oyster, and chanterelle, cut into ⅛-inch slices

1. In bowl, combine dried porcini and 1½ cups hot water. Let sit until soft, about 15 minutes. Remove from liquid. Carefully pour off liquid, leaving sediment in bowl; reserve liquid. Coarsely chop porcini.
2. Chop together garlic, parsley, and kosher salt. Make crostini by grilling bread or toasting it under broiler. Brush lightly with extra-virgin olive oil. Season with salt and pepper.
3. In a large sauté pan, heat 1 tablespoon butter and 1 tablespoon oil over medium-low heat. Add porcini, shallots, and thyme; cook, stirring often, until shallots wilt, about 10 minutes. Season well with salt and pepper. Add wine, and cook over medium-high heat until liquid is almost completely reduced, 5 to 7 minutes. Add reserved porcini liquid, and cook until almost completely reduced again, 5 to 7 minutes. Remove from heat, transfer to a small bowl, and set aside.
4. Rinse skillet, dry, and return to high heat. Starting with the firmest, cook the mushrooms in two batches, using a tablespoon of butter and a tablespoon of oil for each batch. Season well with salt and pepper, and reduce the heat to medium. Cook, stirring often, until the mushrooms are nearly tender, 5 to 10 minutes. Keep in a large bowl while second batch cooks.
5. Return all the mushrooms to the pan. Add porcini and parsley mixtures. Cook over medium-high heat until garlic gives off an aroma, 2 to 3 minutes. Adjust the seasonings, and remove pan from heat.
6. Transfer mushrooms to a bowl. Serve along with crostini, or spoon a bit of the mushroom mixture on each crostini slice.

Baba Ghanoush

makes 4½ cups

The seasonings can be adjusted to make this smoky spread as strong or as mild as you wish.

6 medium eggplants, about 1¼ pounds each
1 clove garlic, peeled and finely chopped
5 tablespoons tahini (sesame paste)
¼ cup freshly squeezed lemon juice
3 teaspoons salt
2 pinches freshly ground pepper
   Chopped flat-leaf parsley, for garnish

1. Place each eggplant directly over the flame of a gas burner or under a broiler, turning occasionally, until skin is lightly charred, 8 to 10 minutes. Transfer to baking sheet; roast for about 30 minutes in a 425° oven, or until eggplants have shriveled and feel very soft when pressed. Let sit until cool enough to handle.
2. Slit each eggplant open, and remove seeds (don't worry if you miss a few). Scrape flesh from skin with a table knife; transfer to a large bowl. Some charred skin may remain. Discard skin and seeds.
3. Mash the eggplant with a fork, or whisk until fairly smooth but still has a few lumps. Mix in the garlic, tahini, and lemon juice. Add salt and pepper. Adjust flavors as desired. Garnish with chopped parsley. Serve at room temperature.

Fig-and-Prosciutto Sandwiches

makes 32

Mascarpone cheese is available at Italian groceries; if you can't find it, substitute cream cheese.

   8 *thin slices whole-grain bread*
   1 *cup mascarpone cheese*
   8 *ripe green figs, stemmed*
   8 *thin slices prosciutto (about 4 ounces), trimmed of fat and torn into quarters*
  32 *fresh mint leaves*

1. Remove crusts from bread; cut each slice into 4 squares. Spread mascarpone or cream cheese on each square.
2. Cut each fig lengthwise into 4 slices. Place a folded prosciutto slice on each square. Top with mint leaf and slice of fig.

Mock Spit-Roasted Chicken

serves 15

For a very juicy, tender chicken, use the rotisserie attachment on your grill.

   3 *three-pound chickens, preferably organically raised*
   ½ *cup olive oil, plus more for grill*
      Salt and freshly ground pepper

1. Heat oven to 325°. Wash the chickens inside and out with cold water, and pat dry. Rub with oil, and season inside and out with salt and pepper. Roast the chickens on an oven rack until an instant-read thermometer reads 165°, about 1 hour and 20 minutes. Don't allow the chickens to brown.
2. Meanwhile, heat grill until medium hot, adding wood chips for a smoky flavor. Brush the grill with oil. Remove chickens from oven; drain juices from the cavities. Grill, covered, turning often, until golden brown on all sides, about 15 minutes. Carve and serve.

ABOVE: Bite-size sandwiches of prosciutto and sliced fig are enlivened with mascarpone cheese and mint leaves.

Mediterranean-inspired dishes grace this Napa Valley buffet: grilled artichokes, fennel, beets; a trio of salsas; leg of lamb; and green salad. Ease, not perfection, is the aim, as displayed by the simple charm of the table setting, with plenty of napkins and forks ready to be grabbed.

Roast Leg of Lamb

serves 16

A juicy leg of lamb carved into small pieces can be the centerpiece of a buffet.

1 leg of lamb, 6 to 9 pounds
3 large cloves garlic, peeled and slivered
¼ cup olive oil
¼ cup freshly squeezed lemon juice
½ tablespoon dried oregano leaves
2 tablespoons fresh rosemary, coarsely chopped, plus 2 small bunches rosemary sprigs
Salt and freshly ground pepper

1. Remove the papery skin, or fell, from lamb, and trim the fat on top side to ⅝ inch thick. Remove all the fat from bottom side of leg. (You can have your butcher do this.) With the tip of a sharp knife, cut slits in flesh on top and bottom of lamb; insert garlic slivers.
2. Combine the oil, lemon juice, oregano, chopped rosemary, and salt and pepper to taste in small mixing bowl. Rub the lamb well with half the marinade, and refrigerate, covered, for several hours or overnight. Set aside remaining marinade.
3. Remove lamb from refrigerator one hour before you are ready to cook it. Heat oven to 450°. Arrange the rosemary sprigs along both sides of leg, and secure rosemary in three places with butcher's twine. Season well with salt and pepper. Place in roasting pan.
4. Place lamb in oven; turn down heat to 325°. Baste often with remaining marinade. Drain fat from pan periodically. Roast lamb until an instant-read thermometer reads 135° when inserted into thickest part for medium rare, about 1 hour and 20 minutes, or continue cooking to the desired doneness. Untie lamb; let rest 15 minutes before slicing. Carve and serve with condiments and pita.

Honeyed Onions With Currants

makes 1 cup

This condiment can be made a day or two ahead of time; warm before serving.

2 large Spanish onions
1 tablespoon unsalted butter
3 tablespoons honey
1 tablespoon balsamic vinegar
Freshly ground pepper
2 tablespoons dried currants

Peel and cut onions in half lengthwise; slice into ¼-inch-thick semicircles. Place in large skillet with butter, 1¼ cups water, honey, vinegar, and pepper to taste. Bring to a boil, and cook over medium-low heat until most of the liquid has evaporated and onions are very soft, about 40 minutes. Continue to cook until onions are a deep golden brown, about 15 minutes more. Add water as needed to keep onions from scorching. Stir in the currants, and serve.

Grilled Vegetables

serves 10 to 15

4 bulbs fennel, cut into quarters lengthwise and skewered
2 bunches thin carrots, scrubbed
2 bunches beets, peeled and sliced
10 baby artichokes, boiled until tender and cut in half
2 heads radicchio, quartered and skewered
Olive oil for brushing
Salt and freshly ground pepper

Heat grill to medium hot. Brush vegetables with oil, and season with salt and pepper. Grill all vegetables except the radicchio for 10 or 15 minutes, or until tender. Grill radicchio for 2 to 3 minutes. Serve warm or at room temperature.

Roasted-Corn Salsa

makes 5½ cups

Roasting intensifies the corn's sweetness.

4 ears fresh corn, husked
2 tablespoons unsalted butter, melted
5 ripe tomatoes, seeded and cut into quarter-inch dice
½ small red onion, peeled and finely chopped
1 small jalapeño pepper, finely chopped, or to taste
1 small clove garlic, peeled and finely chopped
½ cup cilantro leaves, coarsely chopped
3 tablespoons freshly squeezed lime juice, plus more to taste
Salt and freshly ground pepper

1. Brush corn with melted butter, and place on medium-hot grill or under a broiler, turning often, until about half the kernels are brown, 15 to 20 minutes. Remove corn from heat; let cool. Using a sharp knife, cut kernels from cobs.
2. Combine the corn, tomatoes, onion, jalapeño, garlic, and cilantro in a medium bowl. Season to taste with lime juice, salt, and pepper.

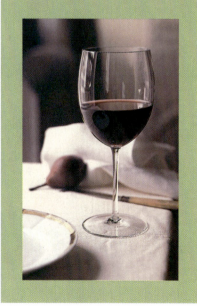

Ice-Cream Sandwiches

makes 24

For best results, prepare sandwiches the day before serving.

- 2 cups plus 2 tablespoons all-purpose flour
- 2 tablespoons unsweetened cocoa
- 5 ounces best-quality semisweet chocolate
- 4 ounces best-quality unsweetened chocolate
- ¾ cup unsalted butter
- 1 teaspoon salt
- 1½ cups sugar
- 3 large eggs, at room temperature
- 1 pint each strawberry, vanilla, and chocolate ice cream

1. Combine flour and cocoa; set aside. Melt together chocolates and butter in a medium bowl set over simmering water. Stir with a wooden spoon until smooth. Add salt and sugar, stirring until sugar is almost completely dissolved, about 5 minutes. Remove bowl from heat. Beat in eggs one at a time, then fold in flour mixture until well combined. Let dough cool slightly in bowl; it will be very soft. Divide into quarters, and spoon onto plastic wrap. Flatten each piece of dough with a wooden spoon, wrap well; refrigerate for at least 2 hours or overnight.

2. When dough is firm, cut each piece in half. Cover a work surface with plastic wrap. Place piece of dough on plastic, and cover with another sheet; roll out to a thickness of ⅛ inch. Keeping dough in plastic, transfer to a baking sheet; place in freezer. Repeat until all dough is rolled out. Stack sheets of dough in freezer; chill until very firm, about 30 minutes.

3. Heat oven to 350°. Line a baking sheet with parchment paper. Remove sheets of dough from freezer one at a time. Place on a parchment-lined work surface, and peel off plastic wrap. Using a 2½-inch-round cookie cutter, cut out dough, and transfer circles to baking sheet. Work quickly to prevent dough from becoming too soft.

4. Bake until cookies are firm to the touch, 14 to 16 minutes, turning baking sheet halfway through baking. Remove from oven; let cookies cool slightly on pan.

Transfer to a wire rack to cool completely.

5. While cookies are baking, transfer ice cream (working with one flavor at a time) to the bowl of an electric mixer fitted with a paddle attachment. Place ice cream in refrigerator to soften slightly, about 15 minutes. Beat ice cream on medium-high speed until soft enough to spread, about 2 minutes, or beat with a wooden spoon. Set bowl in a second bowl filled with ice. Spoon some softened ice cream onto a cookie and top with another cookie. Place sandwich in freezer and continue process. After the ice cream has rehardened, wrap sandwiches tightly in plastic wrap. Serve or freeze overnight.

ABOVE: Strawberries with stems attached can be nibbled through-out the evening or served along with the ice-cream sandwiches.

ABOVE: Ice-cream sandwiches of homemade chocolate cookies and strawberry, vanilla, or chocolate ice cream are a cool, simple treat to finish the buffet. Make the sandwiches ahead of time, and, since they will keep in the freezer, be sure to make plenty of extras so you can enjoy them for days after the party.

BIG TEXAS
BARBECUE

PULLED-CHICKEN AND CORN TAMALES

EMPANADAS WITH SPICY PORK

AVOCADO ENCHILADAS

GRILLED QUAIL AND RIB-EYE STEAK

WEST TEXAS BAKED BEANS

GRILLED RED-POTATO SALAD WITH
WARM BACON VINAIGRETTE

BARBECUED PORK RIBS WITH MAPLE RUB

BEEF TACOS WITH PICO DE GALLO

BUÑUELOS WITH VANILLA ICE CREAM
AND CACTUS BERRIES

OPPOSITE, CLOCKWISE FROM TOP LEFT: The stark setting of the Chinati Foundation in Marfa, Texas, stands in bold contrast to the vivacious party that is thrown there. The Texas−style barbecue begins with Lone Star beer, traditional margaritas, and appetizers in the courtyard. Forks and spoons stand ready in glasses; oversize striped napkins draped over chair backs invite guests to sit right down. Big jars of pickled cucumbers, jalapeños, and onions perch on a ledge.

A big old horse arena in an old cattle town calls for a traditional Texas barbecue on a grand scale, complete with mariachi band.

One of the pleasures of a barbecue is that everything about it is big: the quantity of food, the size of the grill, the number of guests, the sky overhead. Marfa, Texas, an old cattle town with a population of 2,500, is situated deep in barbecue country. There, Donald Judd, the minimalist artist who died in 1994, established an art museum, the Chinati Foundation. One of the buildings is an old concrete horse arena, which Judd renovated and used for dinner parties, as does Marianne Stockebrand, the artist's companion for the last four years of his life and the director of the foundation. Judd designed the grill to serve crowds of people—friends, relatives, and business acquaintances. (A barbecue is the kind of affair that almost begs for extra guests, by the dozens—just toss more food on the grill.) Unlike more formal sit-down dinners, barbecues often provoke gargantuan appetites in otherwise picky eaters. Perhaps it is the aromas wafting off the grill, the sensuous anticipation of the feast as guests watch steaks and quail being turned, and the sight of ribs cooking slowly over mesquite wood. This evening, Stockebrand serves tiny Mexican enchiladas and tacos as appetizers, barbecued meats and poultry as the main course. Guests sit down to eat at utilitarian pine tables—as minimal as the food is extravagant. Throughout the evening, a mariachi band plays tunes from south of the border.

TOP, LEFT TO RIGHT: Margaritas are made with one-third lime juice, one-third tequila, and one-third Triple Sec, cut with a little water and served straight up with salt on the rims. A mariachi trumpet player blows his horn. On the buffet, dinner is served in copper-glazed, clay, and volcanic-stone bowls. ABOVE LEFT: The entire mariachi band performs. OPPOSITE: The chefs agree that a traditional Texas barbecue is all about a hot fire and a good choice of meat; they cook on the huge concrete grill, Martha's favorite barbecue pit.

TOP LEFT: Bite-size pork empanadas served with salsa verde make for colorful appetizers. TOP RIGHT: Pulled-chicken and corn tamales are sliced open and eaten out of the corn husks. ABOVE: The former horse arena now serves as a huge dining hall, an appropriate site for Texas-style entertaining.

Pulled-Chicken and Corn Tamales

makes about 34

In this recipe, corn husks are lined with masa harina, a Mexican corn flour.

44   dried corn husks (see the Guide)
1½ teaspoons cumin seeds
½   teaspoon black peppercorns
1½ teaspoons dried oregano
2   cloves garlic, minced
5   teaspoons salt
¾   cup chipotle chiles in adobo sauce (about half of a 13⅛-ounce can)
2   four-pound roasting chickens
1   tablespoon olive oil
1   onion, finely chopped
¼   teaspoon freshly ground black pepper
2   cups fresh corn kernels (about 4 ears)
3   large tomatoes, cut into ¼-inch dice
1   cup homemade or low-sodium canned chicken stock
1   cup loosely packed cilantro leaves, finely chopped
6   cups masa harina (see the Guide)
6   cups warm water

1. Soak corn husks in water for 24 hours.
2. Heat oven to 425°. In heavy skillet over medium-high heat, toast cumin, peppercorns, and oregano, shaking pan often, until aromatic, 2 minutes. Let cool; finely grind. Purée spices, garlic, 1½ teaspoons salt, and chipotles in food processor.
3. Roast chickens for 30 minutes. Remove from oven; brush with spice mixture. Roast until juices run clear when chicken thigh is pierced, another 30 minutes. Let cool.
4. Meanwhile, heat the oil in large skillet over medium heat. Add the onion, 1 teaspoon salt, and pepper; sauté, stirring often, until soft and fragrant, 3 to 5 minutes. Add corn and tomatoes; cook until corn is soft and tomatoes start to break down, 3 to 5 minutes. Transfer to a bowl.
5. Shred the chicken. Add chicken, stock, 1½ teaspoons salt, and cilantro to onion mixture. Toss well, cover; refrigerate.
6. Whisk together masa harina, remaining tablespoon salt, and warm water.

7. Pat husks dry. Set aside 34 best husks; peel remaining into ribbons to use as ties.
8. Working with a few husks at a time, spread about 3 tablespoons of the masa mixture in center of each; mound 2 heaping tablespoons chicken filling on lower third. Fold the husks over, enclosing the filling; tie the ends with husk ribbons.
9. Place the tamales in a steamer basket over boiling water; reduce heat, cover, and steam until masa is cooked and the filling is hot, about 45 minutes. Slice open, and serve in husks.

Empanadas With Spicy Pork

makes 60

1   tablespoon black peppercorns
1   teaspoon dried oregano
1   teaspoon cumin seeds
½   teaspoon whole cloves
1   small cinnamon stick
2   cloves garlic, minced
1   five-pound pork butt
1   tablespoon vegetable oil
2   small onions, finely diced
     Salsa Verde (recipe follows)
2   teaspoons salt
¼   teaspoon freshly ground black pepper
½   cup homemade or low-sodium canned chicken stock
8   cups all-purpose flour
1   cup vegetable shortening
2   tablespoons baking powder
2½   cups warm water
8   tablespoons (1 stick) unsalted butter, melted

1. Toast the spices in small, heavy skillet over medium-high heat, shaking pan often, 2 to 3 minutes. Be careful not to scorch the spices. Let cool, finely grind, and combine with garlic.
2. Heat oven to 425°. Bring pork to room temperature; rub with spice mixture. Roast in a heavy roasting pan until pork is very well done and falling off the bone, about 2½ hours. Let stand until cool

enough to handle. Trim fat, and remove pork from bone. Dice into small pieces, cover, and set aside.
3. Heat oil in large skillet over medium heat. Add onions; sauté, stirring, until soft, about 5 minutes. Add pork, 2 cups Salsa Verde, 1½ teaspoons salt, pepper, and stock. Simmer until liquid starts to thicken, 5 to 8 minutes.
4. Whisk together the flour, shortening, remaining ½ teaspoon salt, and baking powder in bowl. Add warm water; knead dough until smooth. Cover; let stand 10 minutes. Divide into sixty 1½-inch balls; cover with plastic.
5. Lightly flour work surface; roll out each dough ball to 3½-inch disk. Place 1 heaping tablespoon of pork filling in center of each. Fold dough to enclose filling; form half moon. Seal edges, crimping with fork.
6. Heat oven to 425°. Arrange empanadas on parchment-lined baking sheets; generously brush with butter. Bake two pans (meanwhile, refrigerate others) until light brown, 20 to 25 minutes; rotate the pans between racks halfway through. Let cool slightly; bake remaining pans. Serve with remaining Salsa Verde.

Salsa Verde

makes 4 cups

Blanch tomatillos to take away bitterness.

1   pound tomatillos, husks removed
1   cup loosely packed cilantro leaves, roughly chopped
5   jalapeño peppers, diced
6   scallions, chopped
2   cloves garlic, minced
2   tablespoons freshly squeezed lime juice
½   teaspoon salt
⅛   teaspoon freshly ground black pepper

1. Add tomatillos to boiling water; cook 3 to 5 minutes, until just soft. Drain. Let cool; chop into ½-inch pieces.
2. Toss in bowl with remaining ingredients. Refrigerate several hours before serving. Salsa will keep refrigerated for three days.

TOP: Marfa's proximity to Mexico is reflected in the barbecue's menu, which includes avocado enchiladas.
ABOVE: Host Marianne Stockebrand enjoys a margarita while listening to the mariachi music with a guest.

Avocado Enchiladas

serves 12 to 14

2 dried ancho chiles (available at specialty-food stores and many supermarkets)

4 cups plus 1 tablespoon vegetable oil

½ medium onion, cut into ¼-inch dice

2 cloves garlic, minced

2 tablespoons dark-brown sugar

5 tablespoons ground cumin

2 tablespoons dried oregano

2 cups white wine

1 twenty-eight-ounce can crushed plum tomatoes

2 cups homemade or low-sodium canned chicken stock, skimmed of fat

8 Haas avocados

1 cup loosely packed cilantro leaves, roughly chopped

¼ cup freshly squeezed lime juice

¾ teaspoon salt

¼ teaspoon freshly ground black pepper

25 corn tortillas

1½ pounds jack cheese, grated

1. Place the chiles in saucepan; add water to cover. Bring to a boil. Reduce the heat, and simmer 5 to 10 minutes. Cool slightly, remove stems, and purée the chiles and liquid in a food processor.

2. Heat 1 tablespoon oil in a deep skillet over medium heat. Add the onion, garlic, brown sugar, cumin, and oregano; sauté until onion is soft, 4 to 5 minutes. Add wine, chile purée, tomatoes, and stock; simmer about 20 more minutes, until thickened to stew consistency.

3. Peel, pit, and roughly chop the avocados. Toss with the cilantro, lime juice, salt, and pepper.

4. Heat oven to 400°. Heat remaining 4 cups oil in a wide, heavy saucepan over medium heat until very hot but not smoking, 7 to 10 minutes. Using tongs, fry six tortillas, one at a time, for 2 to 3 seconds. Blot on paper towel.

5. Dip fried tortillas in chile sauce to lightly coat both sides. Spoon 2 tablespoons avocado filling onto each tortilla; roll up. Spread ½ cup chile sauce into large, deep casserole. Arrange rolled tortillas in casserole so they fit snugly; repeat entire process, covering bottom of casserole; pour 1 cup sauce over tortillas; sprinkle with half the cheese. Make a second layer using remaining ingredients. Top with remaining sauce and cheese.

6. Bake enchiladas until heated through, 25 to 30 minutes. Serve immediately.

Grilled Quail and Rib-Eye Steak

serves 12 to 14

For a less elaborate spread, serve the quails or steaks on their own.

12 quails (about ½ pound each)

¼ cup plus 3 tablespoons olive oil

½ cup loosely packed thyme leaves

½ teaspoon freshly ground black pepper

12 boneless 1-inch-thick rib-eye steaks

1 tablespoon salt

1. Rinse quails under cold water; pat dry. Arrange in large, shallow baking pan. Add ¼ cup oil, ¼ cup thyme, and ¼ teaspoon pepper to pan; coat quails thoroughly. Cover, and refrigerate, up to 24 hours.

2. Arrange rib-eye steaks in large, shallow baking pan. Add remaining 3 tablespoons oil, ¼ cup thyme, and ¼ teaspoon pepper to pan; coat steaks thoroughly. Cover and refrigerate, up to 24 hours.

3. Return the meat to room temperature. Heat grill to medium hot. Sprinkle steaks and quails with salt. Grill the steaks until seared outside and cooked to the desired doneness inside, 10 to 12 minutes per side for medium rare. Grill quails, breast-side first, until golden brown and cooked through, 12 to 15 minutes per side.

West Texas Baked Beans

6   cups pinto beans (2½ pounds)
1   pound bacon
2   onions, cut into ¼-inch dice
4   teaspoons chile powder
4   cloves garlic, minced
1¼ cups firmly packed light-brown sugar
2   twelve-ounce bottles dark beer
    Salt and freshly ground black pepper

1. In stockpot or Dutch oven, cover beans with six inches cold water. Soak overnight.
2. In skillet, cook bacon over medium heat until crisp. Remove bacon; set aside.
3. Pour off all but 3 tablespoons fat. Add onions, chile powder, and garlic; sauté, stirring, until onions are soft, 5 minutes.
4. Drain beans. Return to stockpot; cover with water by 2 inches. Crumble bacon into small pieces; add to beans with onion mixture, brown sugar, and beer. Cook, covered, over medium-high heat (or on grill); stir occasionally, until beans are soft and liquid is almost absorbed, about 2½ hours. Adjust seasoning.

Grilled Red-Potato Salad With Warm Bacon Vinaigrette

serves 14

10 pounds new potatoes, scrubbed
3   tablespoons salt
1¼ pounds bacon
2   large red onions, sliced into very thin
    semicircles
½   cup olive oil
¼   cup plus 2 tablespoons apple-cider vinegar
1   cup light-brown sugar
¾   teaspoon freshly ground black pepper

1. Add the potatoes and 2 tablespoons salt to large pot of cold water. Bring to boil; boil until almost fork tender. Drain.
2. Cook bacon in skillet until crisp, 5 minutes. Remove bacon, crumble, and set

aside. Pour off all but 2 tablespoons fat.
3. Return skillet to heat; add onions, and cook until soft, 3 to 5 minutes. Add 5 tablespoons oil, vinegar, and sugar; cook, stirring until the sugar dissolves, 3 to 5 minutes. Add 1½ teaspoons salt and ¼ teaspoon pepper.
4. Heat the grill to medium hot. Slice the potatoes in half; toss with the remaining 3 tablespoons oil, 1½ teaspoons salt, and ½ teaspoon pepper. Grill the potatoes until crisp and cooked through, 3 to 4 minutes per side. Return the potatoes to bowl. Add the dressing and bacon; toss. Serve warm or at room temperature.

BELOW: Guests can choose from a broad selection of dishes, according to individual taste; this plate includes a sampling of grilled quail, red-potato salad, and baked beans.

TOP LEFT: The long dinner tables are set with white Buffalo china and enamel utensils; votive candles in paper bags along the walls are lit before guests enter the former horse arena. TOP RIGHT: The beef-and-cabbage tacos are served with pico de gallo. LEFT: The buffet dinner includes grilled corn that was soaked in brine before going on the fire; the rib-eye steaks—a heavily-marbled prime cut—were sliced an inch-and-a-half thick and weighed one pound each before being grilled.

Barbecued Pork Ribs With Maple Rub

serves 12 to 16

Maple sugar, available at specialty-food stores, adds a distinctive taste to this dish, but light-brown sugar can be substituted.

2 pounds maple sugar
¼ cup salt
2 tablespoons paprika
¼ cup freshly ground black pepper
2 tablespoons fresh thyme leaves
4 cloves garlic, minced
   Zest of two lemons
¼ cup olive oil
4 racks pork spareribs (3 pounds each)

1. Combine the sugar, salt, paprika, pepper, thyme, garlic, and zest; spread on a sheet pan; let stand at room temperature overnight so sugar will be hard and dry. Grind in food processor to fine powder.
2. Brush the ribs with oil; coat with sugar.
3. Heat grill to medium hot; grill ribs, fat-side down first, until meat is just coming off bone, 20 to 30 minutes per side. Cool slightly. Slice into individual ribs; serve.

Beef Tacos With Pico de Gallo

makes 14

2 cups masa harina (see the Guide)
2 teaspoons salt
¼ teaspoon baking powder
1 cup plus 3 tablespoons warm water
1 tablespoon vegetable oil
1 small onion, cut into ¼-inch dice
1 pound ground beef
2 large tomatoes, cut into ½-inch dice
1 tablespoon ground cumin
½ tablespoon dried oregano
¼ teaspoon freshly ground black pepper
1 cup shredded green cabbage
   Pico de Gallo (recipe follows)

1. Combine the masa harina, 1 teaspoon salt, and baking powder. Add water; knead together by hand to form smooth dough.
2. Lightly flour a work surface. Pinch off 1½-inch ball of dough; roll into 4-inch disk.
3. Heat a heavy skillet, preferably cast iron, to medium high. Cook disks, one or two at a time, until just puffed and slightly golden, 2 to 3 minutes; turn, and cook 1 to 2 minutes more. Remove from the heat; fold in half to create shell. Repeat with the remaining dough.
4. Heat oil in large skillet over medium-high heat. Add onion; cook until soft, 3 to 5 minutes. Add beef; cook, stirring, until well browned, 5 to 7 minutes. Drain excess fat. Stir in tomatoes, cumin, and oregano; season to taste with pepper and remaining teaspoon salt. Simmer until tomatoes break down and mixture is saucy, 3 to 5 minutes.
5. Fill each shell with 1 tablespoon shredded cabbage and 1 tablespoon beef. Spoon small amount of Pico de Gallo over beef, or serve Pico de Gallo on the side.

Pico de Gallo

makes 3 cups

2 medium tomatoes, cut into ½-inch dice
2 jalapeño peppers, finely chopped
1 small red onion, cut into ¼-inch dice
2 scallions, finely chopped
¼ cup freshly squeezed lime juice
½ cup loosely packed cilantro leaves, roughly chopped
½ teaspoon ground chile powder, preferably pasilla
½ teaspoon salt
⅛ teaspoon freshly ground black pepper

Combine all ingredients in mixing bowl; toss well to combine. Adjust seasoning to taste. Serve immediately or keep refrigerated until serving, up to two days.

don't forget

• The quality of every barbecue starts with the quality of the meat: always buy the best.

• At a barbecue, excess is good. Have more than enough of everything, starting, of course, with food. Don't forget extra cases of chilled beer, as well as pitchers of iced tea and water. Since eating ribs is a deliciously messy business, have plenty of extra napkins.

• If it is hot and sunny, provide hats—big cowboy hats, straw hats, baseball caps—so people can have a little shade. Or rent tables with umbrellas, so guests can savor the aromas coming off the grill without sweltering beneath the sun.

• You can involve your guests in grilling, if they would like to pitch in. They can take turns tending the grill, or cook their own steaks to an exact degree of doneness.

• A barbecue is a country event, so musical selections could include Willie Nelson, Waylon Jennings, Ry Cooder, Dolly Parton, k.d. lang, or Garth Brooks. For a Mexican note, mariachi music, whether live or recorded, will make the party.

ABOVE: Earlier in the afternoon, Martha helped prepare the dessert buñuelos, which are pieces of fried dough that are formed into basket shapes. RIGHT: Cactus berries, which range in color from green to purplish-red, have soft, sweet flesh beneath their prickly skin. OPPOSITE: When serving the buñuelos, scoop vanilla ice cream into the fried dough, then top with fresh cactus berries and cajeta, a caramelized-sugar sauce; fresh raspberries can be used as well.

Buñuelos With Vanilla Ice Cream and Cactus Berries

serves 12

Cactus berries are often called cactus pears or prickly pears. Look for them at specialty-food stores.

    1¼ pounds cactus berries or 1½ pints
         raspberries
     4   cups all-purpose flour
     1   teaspoon salt
     2   teaspoons baking powder
    ¼   cup vegetable oil plus 3 quarts for frying
     1   cup hot water
    ½   cup sugar
     1   tablespoon cinnamon
     2   pints vanilla ice cream
         Cajeta Sauce (recipe follows)

1. Cut away skin of cactus berries. Slice half the cactus berries into ½-inch pieces (if using raspberries, leave whole); purée the remaining berries; toss purée with reserved berries. Cover, and set aside.
2. Sift together flour, salt, and baking powder. Add ¼ cup oil and just enough hot water to bring dough together; knead until smooth and silky. Cover with plastic wrap.
3. Slowly heat frying oil in heavy saucepan or Dutch oven to 365°. Thoroughly combine sugar and cinnamon.
4. Meanwhile, divide dough into twelve 2-inch balls. Roll out each on lightly floured work surface into a 7-inch round. Keep excess dough covered.
5. Carefully drop rolled dough one piece at a time into oil. Dough should sink to bottom of pan, then float to the surface. Using tongs, gently press center of dough, about 20 seconds, to create concave shape; fry until crisp and lightly golden, 2 to 3 minutes. Lift from oil with tongs, allowing oil to drip back into saucepan.
6. Transfer buñuelos to a baking sheet lined with several paper towels. Sprinkle liberally with cinnamon sugar.
7. To serve, scoop ice cream into buñuelos. Top with Cajeta Sauce and berries.

Cajeta Sauce

makes 4 cups

This traditional dessert, made from milk and caramelized sugar, can be served by itself or poured over ice cream or fruit.

     2   cups sugar
    ½   teaspoon salt
     1   tablespoon freshly squeezed lemon juice
    ½   cup goat's milk or heavy cream

1. Combine the sugar, salt, lemon juice, and 1 tablespoon water in a wide, heavy-bottomed saucepan over medium-low heat. Cover saucepan, and cook, checking occasionally until sugar melts and turns amber, 10 to 12 minutes. Do not overcook, or sugar will burn.
2. Remove from heat; slowly whisk in milk. Let cool completely. Drizzle sauce over ice cream, and serve, or store covered in refrigerator up to one week.

VIETNAMESE-THAI FEAST

CRISP SPRING ROLLS

RICE-PAPER-WRAPPED SALAD ROLLS

STIR-FRIED GARDEN VEGETABLES

VIETNAMESE FISHERMAN'S SOUP

FIRECRACKER PRAWNS

GRILLED SHRIMP PASTE ON SUGARCANE

STRIPED BASS WITH GINGER-LIME SAUCE

GRILLED LEMONGRASS CHICKEN

CHUNKY GINGER ICE CREAM

KAFFIR-LIME COCONUT-MACAROON TARTS

OPPOSITE: An oversize square table is created by placing a sheet of plywood over a smaller table; raw silk drapes to the ground, while criss-crossing runners add to the extravagant feel. Padded covers make camp stools more comfortable.

A Vietnamese-Thai dinner is both about exploring the nuances of two cuisines and about the leisure with which it is savored.

"The cooking tends to move fast, but in the eating, everything slows down," says Mai Pham, the founder and proprietor of the Lemon Grass restaurant and cafés in Sacramento, California. Asian cuisines, as well as Asian hospitality, lend themselves to a party for intimates, where trust is implicit and conversation is unguarded. While Pham was growing up in Vietnam, family members and guests would routinely sit at the dinner table for three to four hours, talking throughout the evening and enjoying the relaxed pace. Since no dish is cooked for very long in Vietnamese or Thai traditions, the kitchen would produce a parade of dishes: steaming bowls of soup, a platter of stir-fried vegetables, skewers of beef. In this country, Pham continues to prepare both the herbaceous, rather mild food of Vietnam and the fiery food of Thailand—two distinct yet harmonious cuisines. Lemongrass and lime juice add tartness; ginger, chiles, and curries give fire; coconut milk adds richness; and the essential fish sauce delivers an intriguing saltiness. The contrast of textures and temperatures is splendid, the method of eating a convenient, simple ritual. The meal takes on a slow, spontaneous rhythm as diners take leaves of lettuce, wrap them around piping-hot morsels of grilled meats, dip the little feast into a sauce, and eat. Each small gesture with the hands is done carefully, gracefully, unhurriedly. For Pham, this type of meal is a bridge to her past. For others, who can find the ingredients wherever there are Asian markets or Asian sections in supermarkets, this dinner is a relaxed culinary adventure with intriguing perfumes and unique tastes.

TOP, LEFT TO RIGHT: Chilled black tea with a bamboo-skewered chunk of mango. A small flask of flowers is as delicate and dramatic as the meal's flavors. Host Pham brings out a plate of crisp striped bass and rice. ABOVE LEFT: Thin slices of lemon, which help cut grease and sweeten hands, float in finger bowls.

TOP LEFT: A garden by the American River in Sacramento is the perfect setting for greeting guests with appetizers, chilled black tea, and Napa Valley wines; clear glass decanters display the colors of the tea and wines. TOP RIGHT: Pham serves a fisherman's soup as an intermezzo; floating in the spicy broth are bits of salmon, scallops, and fresh pineapple, a sweet surprise. LEFT: Visions of Southeast Asia are evoked by flowers floating in water bowls and bamboo-shaped candles set on inexpensive wooden trays.

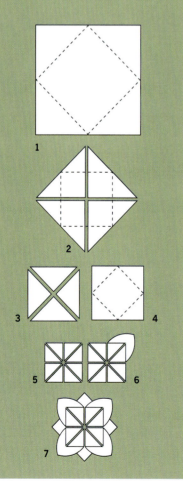
Crisp Spring Rolls

makes 36 to 40

Serve lettuce and herbs on a platter, and wrap the leaves around the spring rolls.

- 1   *ounce green bean-thread vermicelli*
- 1   *tablespoon dried tree-ear or wood-ear mushrooms*
- ½   *cup finely chopped onion*
- 1   *cup finely grated carrots*
- ¼   *cup thinly sliced scallions*
- 2   *large eggs*
- 2   *tablespoons Asian fish sauce*
- 1½ *teaspoons minced garlic*
- 2   *teaspoons sugar*
- ¼   *teaspoon salt*
- ½   *teaspoon freshly ground pepper*
- ½   *pound ground skinless chicken breast*
- ½   *pound ground pork*
- 1   *tablespoon cornstarch*
- 1   *package 8-inch-square fresh or frozen spring-roll wrappers, thawed*
- 3   *cups peanut oil*
- 1   *small head red-leaf lettuce, leaves separated*
- 1   *bunch basil, leaves only*
- 1   *bunch mint, leaves only*
- 1   *bunch cilantro, leaves only*
  Vietnamese Dipping Sauce (recipe on page 54)

1. Place vermicelli in large bowl. Cover with hot water, soak 30 minutes, then drain. Cut into ½-inch lengths. Place dried mushrooms in small bowl. Cover with boiling water, soak 30 minutes, then drain. Roughly chop mushrooms; add to vermicelli with onion, carrots, scallions.

2. Whisk together eggs, fish sauce, garlic, sugar, salt, and pepper. Using a fork, mix chicken and pork into egg mixture. Add noodle mixture; mix until just combined.

3. In a small saucepan over medium heat, whisk cornstarch and 5 tablespoons water until mixture comes to a boil and looks like a smooth porridge, 1 to 2 minutes; remove cornstarch paste from heat.

4. Line a baking sheet with parchment. Stack wrappers neatly; cut in half into 4-by-8-inch rectangles. Loosely cover with plastic wrap. Take one wrapper, and, with the narrow edge facing you, place on a clean surface. Place 1 tablespoon filling ½ inch in from narrow edge. Fold ½ inch of right and left sides over filling, and roll wrapper to form cylinder. Use your index finger to smear cornstarch paste along end of the wrapper; gently press to seal. Transfer to prepared baking sheet. Repeat, using all wrappers and filling.

5. Heat the oil (there should be enough to cover spring rolls) in a wok or large saucepan over medium-high heat to 375° on candy or frying thermometer. (If using a wok, turn burner grate upside down; place wok directly on grate so it is as close to flame as possible.) Carefully slip spring rolls into oil, as many as will fit comfortably. Fry, turning often, until golden and crisp, about 3 minutes. Using a slotted spoon, transfer spring rolls to paper towels to drain. Repeat until all rolls are cooked. Serve immediately. To eat, sprinkle inside of a lettuce leaf with herb leaves, wrap lettuce around a spring roll, and dip in Vietnamese Dipping Sauce.

Chopstick rests are reeds wrapped in silver threads; the stem of a wax orange blossom is tucked into more silver threads holding the chopsticks together; a folded napkin echoes the floating flower.

A square green plate makes a perfect background for salad rolls, dipping sauce, and delicious *chao tom*—lengths of sugarcane covered with a shrimp-and-onion paste, first steamed, then lightly grilled.

Rice-Paper-Wrapped Salad Rolls

serves 8

Salad rolls can be made several hours in advance and stored at room temperature in an airtight container lined with dampened cheesecloth. Do not refrigerate or rice paper will toughen.

- *2 ounces rice vermicelli*
- *2 teaspoons salt*
- *1 boneless, skinless chicken breast (12 ounces), split*
- *16 medium shrimp*
- *1 package 12-inch round rice papers*
- *1 cup bean sprouts*
- *½ cup packed mint leaves, plus more for garnish*
- *8 large or 16 small red-leaf lettuce leaves, cut in half lengthwise*
- *¼ cup finely chopped roasted peanuts*
- *2 tablespoons ground-chile paste*
  Peanut-Hoisin Sauce (recipe on page 54)
  Vietnamese Dipping Sauce (recipe on page 54)

1. Add rice vermicelli and 1 teaspoon salt to boiling water; cook until al dente, about 3 minutes. Drain, rinse, and set aside.

2. Add chicken and remaining teaspoon salt to boiling water. Reduce heat to medium high; simmer the chicken until it is cooked through, about 10 minutes. Remove chicken from water; reserve the water. Slice chicken across the grain ⅛ inch thick, and set aside.

3. Return water to a boil. Add shrimp; reduce heat to medium high. Cook shrimp until opaque, 2 to 3 minutes. Drain. When cool, remove shells. Cut each shrimp in half lengthwise, devein, and set aside.

4. Fill a pan large enough to hold the rice paper with hot water. Dampen a clean kitchen towel with water; spread it out on a clean surface. Immerse 1 sheet of rice paper in the hot water until softened and flexible, about 1 minute. Transfer to dampened towel and smooth out. Fold paper in by 2 inches on both right and left sides. Place 4 shrimp halves in a row, cut-side up, 2 inches from bottom edge; top with 2 to 3 slices chicken. Place 1 heaping tablespoon vermicelli on top, and sprinkle with about 1 tablespoon bean sprouts. Cover with 5 to 6 mint leaves. Place 1 or 2 pieces of lettuce, curly sides out, on top. Fold bottom edge of rice paper over filling; roll up tightly to form a cylinder about 1½ inches in diameter. Repeat until all ingredients are used.

5. Cut rolls into two or four pieces, and arrange on a serving platter. Top with peanuts and dabs of chile paste; garnish with mint leaves. Serve with Peanut-Hoisin Sauce and Vietnamese Dipping Sauce.

RIGHT: Pham uses commercially produced rice paper to wrap salad rolls; the traditional woven pattern pressed into the paper harks back to a time when Vietnamese women dried homemade rice paper on baskets. (1) Rice papers are softened in warm water. (2) Two sides are folded in, forming a long rectangle. Fillings are layered on at one end, beginning with shrimp. (3) Next, add chicken, rice noodles, bean sprouts, mint leaves, and, finally, a leaf of crisp red-leaf lettuce. (4) Roll the rice-paper pancake into a neat cylinder; use a sharp knife to cut into four pieces.

Peanut-Hoisin Sauce

makes 1¾ cups

Hoisin sauce tastes better when mixed with other ingredients. This is also good as a marinade for fish, chicken, or beef.

- 1 *cup hoisin sauce*
- ¼ *cup rice-wine vinegar*
- ⅓ *cup finely minced yellow onion*
- 1 *tablespoon ground-chile paste, or to taste*
- 1 *tablespoon finely chopped roasted peanuts*

Combine ½ cup water, hoisin sauce, vinegar, and onion in saucepan; bring to a boil over medium-high heat. Reduce heat to low; simmer until onions have softened, 7 to 9 minutes. If sauce becomes too thick, add water. Let cool. Transfer to serving dish; top with chile paste and peanuts.

Vietnamese Dipping Sauce

makes 1½ cups

Known as *nuoc cham*, this table sauce is used in almost every Vietnamese dish.

- 1½ *teaspoons minced garlic*
- 1 *teaspoon ground-chile paste*
- 1 *Thai chile or serrano pepper, chopped, optional*
- ¼ *cup Asian fish sauce*
- 2 *tablespoons freshly squeezed lime juice*
- ¼ *cup sugar*
- 2 *tablespoons grated carrots, for garnish*

With a mortar and pestle, pound garlic, chile paste, and fresh chile into a paste (or mince together with a knife). It is best to wear plastic gloves so that the chiles don't burn; be sure not to rub your eyes after chopping. Transfer to a bowl. Add fish sauce, ⅔ cup hot water, lime juice, and sugar. Whisk together until sugar dissolves. Serve sprinkled with carrots.

Stir-Fried Garden Vegetables

serves 8

- ½ *pound Asian long beans or green beans, cut into 3-inch lengths*
- 1 *pound flowering Chinese mustard or broccoli rabe, cut into 3-inch lengths*
- 2 *tablespoons vegetable oil*
- 3 *medium cloves garlic, thinly sliced*
- 1 *small onion, peeled and cut lengthwise ¼ inch thick*
- ½ *yellow bell pepper, cut into ¼-inch strips*
- ½ *red bell pepper, cut into ¼-inch strips*
- 1½ *tablespoons oyster sauce*

1. Cook beans and Chinese mustard in boiling water until bright green and crisp, for 2 to 3 minutes. Cool in ice water; drain.
2. In a wok or a large nonstick skillet, heat oil over high heat. Add garlic and onion; cook, stirring, until they begin to brown, about 1 minute. Add the beans, Chinese mustard, peppers, and oyster sauce; cook, stirring, until tender, about 2 minutes. Serve immediately.

Vietnamese Fisherman's Soup

serves 8

You can use any kind of seafood you like in this sweet-and-spicy soup.

- ½ *pound boneless, skinless salmon, cut into bite-size pieces*
- ¼ *pound bay scallops, muscles removed*
- 1 *tablespoon vegetable oil*
- 1 *teaspoon ground-chile paste*
- 1 *teaspoon minced garlic*
- 5 *cups homemade or canned low-sodium chicken stock, skimmed of fat*
- 2 *ripe tomatoes (1 pound), cored and cut into ½-inch dice*
- 2 *cups diced fresh pineapple*
- ½ *medium onion, sliced lengthwise ¼ inch thick*
- 2 *tablespoons Asian fish sauce*
- ¼ *cup sugar*
- ¼ *teaspoon salt*
- ¼ *cup freshly squeezed lime juice*
- 3 *scallions, white and light-green parts only, cut diagonally ¼ inch thick*
- 2 *cups bean sprouts*
- 2 *tablespoons chopped sweet basil*
- 2 *tablespoons chopped cilantro*
- 2 *tablespoons Fried Shallots (recipe follows), optional*

1. Blanch salmon in boiling water for 10 to 20 seconds. Lift out; drain in colander. Blanch scallops for 10 seconds; drain.
2. Heat oil in a small stockpot over medium heat. Add chile paste and garlic. Cook until fragrant, about 10 seconds. Add the stock, cover, and bring to a boil. Reduce heat to medium; stir in salmon, scallops, tomatoes, pineapple, onions, fish sauce, sugar, salt, and lime juice. Cook just until seafood is cooked through, about 3 to 5 minutes. Remove from heat, stir in the scallions, bean sprouts, basil, and cilantro. Divide among 8 soup bowls, and garnish with Fried Shallots, if desired. Serve immediately.

Fried Shallots

makes ⅔ cup

4 to 5 medium shallots, thinly sliced
1 cup vegetable oil

1. Spread shallots on a paper-towel-lined baking sheet; let dry for 15 to 20 minutes.
2. Heat oil in small heavy skillet over medium-low heat. Test by dropping a shallot slice into bubbling oil. If shallot floats to surface, oil is ready. Stir in all shallots; fry until golden, stirring often, 4 to 6 minutes. Remove with slotted spoon; drain on paper towels. Sprinkle into Vietnamese Fisherman's Soup.

Firecracker Prawns

serves 8

4 large shallots, peeled
1 pound large shrimp
3 tablespoons cornstarch
½ teaspoon paprika
1½ teaspoons coarse salt
½ teaspoon coarsely cracked black pepper
3 tablespoons vegetable oil
1 teaspoon minced garlic
1 teaspoon sugar
1 teaspoon Asian fish sauce
¼ cup thinly sliced red or yellow bell
    pepper
2 scallions, sliced diagonally ½ inch long
1 fresh serrano or ½ jalapeño pepper,
    thinly sliced
½ teaspoon whole black peppercorns
½ teaspoon whole white peppercorns
3 sprigs cilantro, for garnish

1. Thinly slice two shallots; set aside. Finely chop remaining two shallots. Using kitchen shears, cut through backs of shrimp shells. Leaving shells on, use a small sharp knife to devein shrimp.
2. Carefully lift one side of each shrimp shell; tuck ½ teaspoon chopped shallot into each shrimp. Gently press all the shells back in place.
3. In a large bowl, combine the corn-starch, paprika, salt, and cracked pepper. Add the shrimp; toss to coat thoroughly.
4. In a large nonstick skillet, heat oil over medium-high heat. Add shrimp; cook just until opaque, about 2 minutes on each side. Scatter garlic and reserved sliced shallots over shrimp, and cook, shaking pan often, 1 minute. Add the sugar, fish sauce, 3 tablespoons water, bell pepper, scallions, serrano pepper, and black and white peppercorns; toss to combine. Cook, shaking pan often, 1 minute. Garnish with cilantro, and serve immediately.

BELOW: The firecracker prawns are worthy of their name: Black and white peppercorns and a serrano pepper season the shrimp, along with paprika, garlic, and fish sauce.

Grilled Shrimp Paste on Sugarcane

makes 12

1   tablespoon vegetable oil
¼   cup finely chopped yellow onion
½   cup finely chopped shallots
1   pound shrimp, peeled and deveined
2   teaspoons Asian fish sauce
¼   teaspoon salt
1   tablespoon sugar
1   teaspoon minced garlic
½   teaspoon freshly ground white pepper
2   tablespoons cornstarch
½   teaspoon paprika
½   teaspoon baking powder
2   scallions, white and light-green parts only, finely chopped
3   six-inch pieces sugarcane, fresh or canned, cut lengthwise into quarters
*   Scallion Oil (recipe follows), optional*

1. In skillet, heat oil over low heat. Add onion and shallots; cook, stirring occasionally, until translucent, 6 to 7 minutes.
2. In food processor, pulse shrimp to textured paste, about 20 pulses. Transfer to bowl; add onion mixture, fish sauce, salt, sugar, garlic, pepper, cornstarch, paprika, baking powder, and scallions. Stir to combine. Cover; refrigerate for 30 minutes.
3. Lightly brush a baking sheet with oil. Dampen your hands with cold water; shape 2 tablespoons shrimp paste into a ball. Hold shrimp paste in one hand, and press a piece of sugarcane into it, enclosing center of sugarcane but leaving about 1½ inches exposed at top and bottom. Set aside on prepared baking sheet. Repeat.
4. Brush a bamboo or metal steamer basket with oil; place over boiling water in a wide saucepan or wok. Steam sugarcane sticks, covered, until shrimp is opaque, 4 to 5 minutes. They may be prepared up to this point 6 hours in advance; refrigerate until about 15 minutes before ready to serve.
5. Brush a grill or grill pan with oil; heat until hot. Grill sticks until lightly charred all over, 5 to 8 minutes. Brush with Scallion Oil, if desired, and serve.

Scallion Oil

makes ⅔ cup

In Vietnam, this oil is brushed on rice noodles or grilled meats, or used as a topping for rice dishes.

5   scallions, sliced ¼ inch thick
½   cup vegetable oil

In a small saucepan over medium-low heat, simmer the scallions and vegetable oil gently for 10 minutes. Store at room temperature for up to three days, or refrigerate for a week. Return the oil to room temperature before serving.

Striped Bass With Ginger-Lime Sauce

serves 8

3   medium cloves garlic, peeled
3   Thai chiles or 2 serrano peppers
1   one-and-a-half-inch piece fresh ginger, peeled
½   teaspoon ground-chile paste, or to taste
2   tablespoons Asian fish sauce
1   tablespoon freshly squeezed lime juice
2   tablespoons sugar
4   eight-ounce boneless striped-bass fillets, skin on
2   tablespoons vegetable oil
2   scallions, julienned
½   medium carrot, julienned
5   sprigs cilantro

1. Smash one garlic clove, and halve one chile lengthwise. Grate 1-inch piece ginger. Mix these with chile paste on a cutting board; mince together to form a paste; transfer to a bowl. Stir in fish sauce, lime juice, sugar, and 2 tablespoons water. Thinly slice remaining chiles diagonally; julienne remaining ginger; add to bowl. Thinly slice remaining garlic; set aside.
2. Cut fillets in half crosswise. In a large nonstick skillet, heat oil over high heat. Add fillets, skin-side down; scatter sliced garlic over fish. Cook until just cooked through and very crisp on the outside, 2 to 3 minutes per side. Transfer to a platter; pour sauce over fish; sprinkle with the scallions, carrots, and cilantro.

Grilled Lemongrass Chicken

serves 8

6 *large stalks lemongrass*
4 *teaspoons Asian fish sauce*
4 *teaspoons soy sauce*
4 *teaspoons sugar*
4 *teaspoons minced garlic*
1 *tablespoon freshly squeezed lemon juice*
¼ *cup vegetable oil*
4 *whole boneless, skinless chicken breasts (about 4 pounds), split*

1. Trim the lemongrass to 5 inches from base; remove bad outer leaves; cut into ½-inch lengths. In a food processor, process lemongrass to a hairlike texture. Place in a bowl; add all the remaining ingredients except chicken.
2. Remove the tenderloins (small piece of meat attached to each breast) from the chicken. Pound the breasts ⅛ inch thick; add with tenderloins to marinade, turning to coat. Marinate, refrigerated, from 30 minutes to 8 hours.
3. Brush a grill or grill pan with oil; heat until medium hot. Grill chicken until cooked through and juices run clear when pierced, 3 to 4 minutes on each side.

Chunky Ginger Ice Cream

makes 1 quart

1 *cup milk*
3 *cups heavy cream*
1 *cup sugar*
1 *tablespoon freshly grated ginger*
   Pinch of salt
6 *large egg yolks*
   Ice water for bath
⅓ *cup finely chopped candied ginger, plus more for garnish*
1 *teaspoon pure vanilla extract*
½ *teaspoon freshly squeezed lemon juice*

1. Bring milk, cream, ½ cup sugar, fresh ginger, and salt to a gentle boil over medium heat; turn off heat.
2. In bowl of electric mixer, whisk the egg yolks and the remaining ½ cup sugar on medium-high speed until thick and fluffy, 3 to 5 minutes.
3. Add half the milk mixture to egg-yolk mixture; whisk to blend. Stir into milk in pan; cook over medium-low heat, stirring with a wooden spoon, until mixture coats back of spoon, 3 to 4 minutes.
4. Remove from heat, pour into a bowl, and place in an ice-water bath to chill, stirring often. Stir in candied ginger, vanilla, and lemon juice. Freeze in an ice-cream maker, following manufacturer's instructions. Serve topped with candied ginger strips, if desired.

ABOVE: Stalks of lemongrass garnish grilled chicken breasts flavored with a soy-lemongrass marinade. The dish is served with the stir-fried garden vegetables, including Asian long beans, flowering Chinese mustard, and red and yellow bell peppers. OPPOSITE: At an Asian meal, when spoons or fingers aren't appropriate for the dish, try chopsticks, which come in various shapes—thin or thick, long or short, blunt or pointed—and are made of a variety of materials, including bamboo, wood, or silver.

Kaffir-Lime Coconut-Macaroon Tarts

makes 12

4 lemons

2 limes

7 large eggs

1½ cups plus 2 tablespoons sugar

3 tablespoons unsalted butter, cut into
small pieces
Ice water for bath

8 ounces flaked sweetened coconut

1 tablespoon honey

1 teaspoon pure vanilla extract

¾ cup sifted all-purpose flour

¾ teaspoon minced fresh kaffir-lime leaves,
optional, plus more for garnish

1. Grate zest from the lemons and limes; squeeze juice into separate bowls. In a stainless-steel bowl, whisk zests, ½ cup lemon juice, 2 tablespoons lime juice, 3 eggs, and ½ cup plus 2 tablespoons sugar. Separate 1 egg; add yolk to egg mixture. Place white in a stainless-steel bowl, cover, and refrigerate. Whisk egg-sugar mixture until slightly thick, 3 to 5 minutes.

2. Place bowl over, not in, simmering water; cook, stirring constantly, until mixture starts to thicken, 8 to 12 minutes. Strain into bowl. Stir in butter until melted. Place bowl in ice-water bath. Let stand, stirring frequently, until cold, 30 to 45 minutes. Refrigerate this lime curd while you make the tart shells.

3. Meanwhile, fold a 10-by-12-inch piece of aluminum foil in quarters. Fold long sides in by 1 inch, press flat, then fold in by ¾ inch, and leave standing for sides. Pinch ends closed; fold by ¼ inch to seal, making canoe-shaped mold 5 inches long and 2 inches wide. Repeat to make 12 molds.

4. Heat oven to 325°. Spread coconut on baking sheet; toast until lightly browned, stirring frequently, 15 to 20 minutes. Cool on a wire rack. Raise oven heat to 350°.

5. Separate remaining 3 eggs. Add whites to bowl with reserved white. Add one cup sugar, honey, and vanilla; whisk together. Place bowl over, not in, simmering water.

Cook, whisking constantly, until warm to touch and sugar dissolves, 2 to 4 minutes.

6. In bowl of electric mixer, beat egg-white mixture on high speed until stiff peaks form, 6 to 8 minutes. Using rubber spatula, fold in toasted coconut, flour, and minced leaves. Use pastry bag to pipe mixture into foil molds, filling them flush with edges. With dampened finger, press well in center about 4 inches long.

7. Place filled molds on baking sheet. Bake until golden brown, 15 to 20 minutes. Let stand on a wire rack until cool before removing foil; cool shells completely before filling with lime curd.

8. Press centers of shells back down. Fill each with 1 tablespoon lime curd. Serve immediately or refrigerate up to 1 hour.

ABOVE: Scoops of ginger ice cream studded with candied ginger are served in pale ceramic dessert bowls. OPPOSITE: A boat-shaped coconut macaroon shell is filled with lime curd and garnished with kaffir-lime leaves. Both the shells and curd may be made up to two days ahead and refrigerated, and then assembled before serving.

SEASIDE DINNER

GRILLED QUESADILLAS

SHRIMP-AND-PROSCIUTTO SPIEDINI

SCALLOP-AND-ORANGE SPIEDINI

COUSCOUS SALAD

PLUM UPSIDE-DOWN CAKE

OPPOSITE: To entertain weekend guests at water's edge, all the amenities of an indoor sit-down dinner have been transported outdoors; new and antique kerosene lanterns illuminate the night. ABOVE: Martha with host Kathe Tanous.

For Saturday dinner, the highlight of the weekend, a simple menu allows hosts to focus on the company of their friends.

Moonlight glimmers on the Gulf of Mexico, fireflies flit above dune grasses, and lanterns glow on the dock and table. This seaside evening, at the home of Kathe Tanous and Bob Levenson on the tiny island of Useppa, off Florida's west coast, is carefully orchestrated both to involve weekend guests and to keep them enchanted. Everything has been organized ahead of time: The seafood is marinated and skewered, the oil measured into the lanterns, the table assembled on the dock. Before the sun dips below the horizon, the hosts invite each guest to take something to the dock. In the processional, one person carries the tablecloth and napkins, another the flatware and serving utensils, yet another the wine. The setting and the assembled group of friends create an ambiance so enticing that people linger for hours, knowing that everything, from the quesadilla appetizers to the grilled seafood to the plum upside-down cake, is ready. They sip cocktails while the sun is still up, sit down to dinner as dusk falls, finally finishing with dessert several hours later. The cooking is easy, taking only a few minutes on the grill. Wine is plentiful, and the only music is the simple, rhythmic sound of water against the pier. Best of all, a water's-edge dinner party can be staged anywhere there is water: by a lake, a pond, or even a pool reflecting a border of votive candles.

TOP, LEFT TO RIGHT: During the day, weekend guests are often happiest entertaining themselves with a book or a swim. On breezy evenings, use kerosene lanterns; unlike candles, they won't blow out. A crisp California Sauvignon Blanc complements this menu's grilled seafood. ABOVE LEFT: Host Bob Levenson, far right, joins guests for cocktails and hors d'oeuvres before sunset. OPPOSITE: Borrowing colors from the sea, the table is covered with a striped green-and-white cloth and surrounded by Parisian park chairs painted green; pink roses and snapdragons arranged in low clusters keep guests' views clear.

Grilled Quesadillas

serves 8 as an appetizer

A quick visit to a hot grill leaves these quesadillas crisp and smoky tasting.

- *12   scallions*
- *8   eight-inch-round flour tortillas*
  Vegetable oil, for brushing
- *¾   pound Monterey Jack cheese, grated*
- *1   jalapeño pepper, minced*
- *½   cup cilantro leaves*

1. Heat grill to medium hot, and place grid 4 inches above coals. Brush scallions with oil; grill until lightly marked, 1 to 2 minutes. Set aside.
2. Brush one side of a tortilla with oil. Place oil-side down on a plate. Sprinkle a quarter of the cheese, jalapeño, and cilantro on tortilla. Arrange 3 scallions on top. Top with another tortilla; carefully slide onto grill. Brush top tortilla with oil.
3. When underside is brown and cheese melts, flip over and grill other side.
4. Cut quesadillas into wedges with a knife or scissors. Serve immediately.

Shrimp-and-Prosciutto Spiedini

serves 8

Spiedini are any mix of ingredients cooked on a skewer.

- *¼   cup dry white wine*
- *2   tablespoons freshly squeezed lemon juice*
- *½   cup extra-virgin olive oil, plus more for brushing*
- *2   bunches fresh rosemary*
  Salt and freshly ground pepper
- *32   jumbo shrimp, peeled and deveined*
- *12   slices prosciutto*
- *1   loaf of coarse-textured Italian bread, cut into 1½-inch cubes*

1. Mix together the white wine, the lemon juice, ½ cup oil, a few sprigs of chopped rosemary, and salt and pepper to taste.

Add the shrimp, and marinate for 1 hour.
2. Heat grill to medium hot, and place grid 4 inches above coals. Remove shrimp from marinade, and wrap a third of a piece of prosciutto around middle of each shrimp. Place shrimp on skewers, alternating with bread cubes, tucking a small sprig of rosemary between shrimp and bread. Drizzle remaining marinade over skewers to moisten the bread. Set aside until ready to grill.
3. Brush with oil, and grill for 2 to 3 minutes on each side.

Scallop-and-Orange Spiedini

serves 8

Prepare half the skewers with laurel leaves and half with thyme.

- *2   pounds large sea scallops, rinsed*
- *¼   cup freshly squeezed orange juice*
- *2   tablespoons freshly squeezed lime juice*
- *½   cup extra-virgin olive oil*
  Salt and freshly ground pepper
- *1   large bunch thyme*
- *5   small oranges, cut into eighths*
- *20   laurel (fresh bay) leaves*

1. Remove small muscles from sides of scallops; discard. Combine citrus juices, oil, and salt and pepper to taste. Crush a few sprigs of thyme; add to marinade. Stir in scallops. Marinate for 1 to 3 hours.
2. Heat a grill to medium hot, and place grid 4 inches above coals. Double-skewer scallops, alternating with orange sections. Tuck a sprig of thyme, or skewer a laurel leaf, between each scallop and orange section. Lay skewers in a pan, and pour remaining marinade over them.
3. Grill for 2 to 3 minutes on each side.

ABOVE: Grilled quesadillas can be cut with kitchen scissors, which also make quick work of cutting pitas into sections. OPPOSITE: Shrimp and scallop spiedini, served with couscous salad, make a festive seaside entrée; it is easy to transport them from refrigerator to grill to table while still on their skewers.

Couscous Salad

serves 8

2 cups water
1½ teaspoons salt
2 cups couscous
1 small red onion, diced
2 small cucumbers, peeled if waxy, seeded, and diced
2 ripe tomatoes, seeded and diced
¼ cup currants (optional)
½ cup chopped flat-leaf parsley
  Couscous Dressing (recipe follows)

1. Bring water to a boil; stir in salt and couscous. Remove pan from heat, cover, and let stand 5 minutes. Transfer couscous to a bowl, and break up any clumps.
2. Toss couscous with remaining ingredients. Add dressing, and mix well.

Couscous Dressing

makes 1 cup

¼ cup freshly squeezed lemon juice
¼ cup olive oil
1 tablespoon sugar
1½ teaspoons freshly ground pepper
1½ teaspoons ground ginger
1½ teaspoons salt
1½ teaspoons cinnamon
1½ teaspoons nutmeg
½ teaspoon ground cloves

Whisk together all ingredients in a bowl.

Plum Upside-Down Cake

serves 8 to 10

For the fruit layer:
10 red or purple plums
6 tablespoons unsalted butter
9 tablespoons sugar
½ teaspoon cinnamon

For the cake:
¾ cup flour
1 teaspoon baking powder
  Large pinch of salt
6 tablespoons yellow cornmeal, preferably stone-ground
6 tablespoons unsalted butter, at room temperature
¼ cup almond paste
¼ cup plus 2 tablespoons sugar
3 large eggs, separated
¼ teaspoon pure vanilla extract
¼ teaspoon almond extract
½ cup milk

1. Cut plums into quarters; remove pits. Heat butter in sauté pan over medium heat until sizzling. Add plums; cook 2 to 3 minutes, until well coated and shiny.
2. Add sugar and cinnamon, and stir to coat plums. Cook, stirring frequently, for 10 to 15 minutes, or until plums soften.
3. Remove fruit with a slotted spoon, and transfer to a baking sheet to cool slightly. Remove pan from heat, saving syrup.
4. Butter and flour a 9½-by-2-inch round cake pan. Arrange fruit, cut-edges down, in concentric circles, starting with outside edge. Fit fruit into remaining spaces.
5. Return syrup to medium heat, and boil until very thick with large bubbles. Immediately pour over fruit. Let cool.
6. Heat oven to 350°. Sift together flour, baking powder, and salt. Stir in cornmeal.
7. Put butter in mixer fitted with paddle. Crumble in almond paste; beat. Gradually add ¾ cup sugar; beat until creamy.
8. Add egg yolks, and beat until well combined. Beat in extracts. Add the dry ingredients alternately with milk, beginning and ending with dry ingredients.
9. In clean bowl, whip egg whites until foamy. Gradually sprinkle in 2 tablespoons sugar; beat until soft peaks form. Add a third of whites to batter; mix with whisk. Gently fold in remaining whites.
10. Spread batter over fruit; bake for 1 hour, or until toothpick inserted in center comes out clean. Let cool in pan.
11. Just before serving, place pan over low heat for 1 minute. Run knife around edges to loosen; invert onto serving plate.

ABOVE: The almond-flavored plum upside-down cake has a little cornmeal in the batter, which gives it a pleasantly grainy texture; it is delicious served with vanilla ice cream or whipped cream. To keep it intact, the dessert is carried to the dock in its baking pan and then turned out onto a cake stand.

SKATING
PARTY

THE BEST HOT CHOCOLATE EVER

FIRE-ROASTED CHEESE SANDWICHES

TOMATO-RICE SOUP

OATMEAL CHOCOLATE-CHIP COOKIES

BANANA-SPLIT BROWNIES

HOMEMADE MARSHMALLOWS

OPPOSITE, CLOCKWISE FROM TOP LEFT: A plaid camp blanket is used as a tablecloth for a tailgate buffet. More blankets are on hand to keep skaters warm. Each guest gets a mug tagged with his or her initials for refills of hot tea or cocoa with marshmallows. On the ice, hockey players and figure skaters work up healthy appetites.

After a week of cold nights, a family's pond is finally frozen thick enough for an old-fashioned skating party.

The party starts in the afternoon and lasts until evening. The hosts, Richard and Amelia Baughman, have invited everyone in the hamlet of Etna, New Hampshire, from the tiniest toddler to septuagenarians. The pond on their farm is large enough to accommodate every type and level of skater—speed skaters and wobbly novices all have space. A teenager practices her figure eights, while her friends play a wild game of hockey. This is the way people first skated, in the open air on a frozen pond cleared of snow. To make sure the ice is safe enough for skating—at least eight inches thick—the hosts cut two holes, one at the edge of the pond and one at the center, using a six-foot-long ice chisel. To make the surface smooth, the Baughmans borrowed the fire department's hose and sprayed three thousand gallons of water over the ice the night before the party; a garden hose or portable pump would suffice for smaller areas. To feed the hungry skaters, they prepare tasty variations on favorite childhood foods like tomato-rice soup, grilled-cheese sandwiches, and hot chocolate, and cart it all in their vintage station wagon to the edge of the pond. Warming campfires help thaw cold fingers and toes, and also are perfect for toasting marshmallows made from scratch by the Baughmans—a special treat to end a special winter's day.

TOP, LEFT TO RIGHT: Homemade marshmallows, made the day before the party, are much better than the store-bought kind; speared on twigs, the sweet cubes are ready for toasting over a fire. A hay-bale rest station helps anchor a pole hung with kerosene lanterns, which are lit before dusk. A skater speeds over the ice. ABOVE LEFT: A silvery winter sky provides an ever-changing canopy for the party. OPPOSITE: In an old wheelbarrow, thermoses keep tea, cocoa, and soup hot; aluminum boxes hold hot dogs; buns and condiments are organized in wooden crates; and rolled dish towels serve as generous napkins.

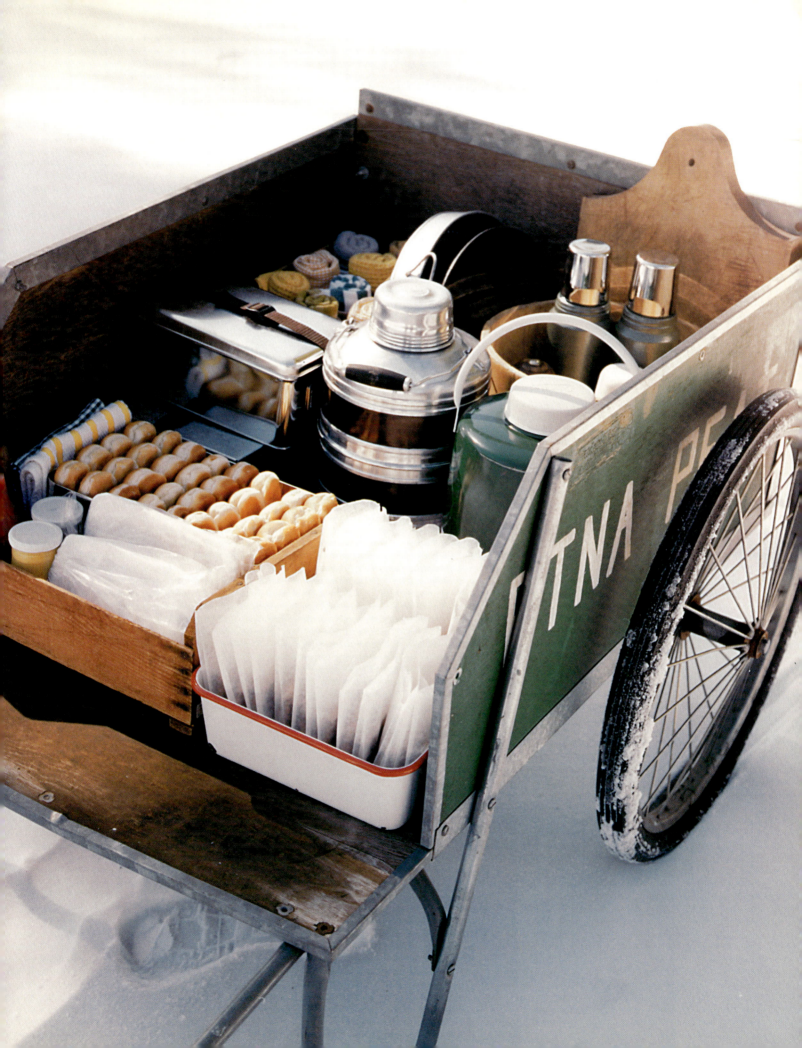

TOP LEFT: As guests arrive at the party, they change into skates and drape their boots over a wooden sawhorse, keeping them out of the snow. TOP RIGHT: For kids, eating hot dogs with the works is the final reward after roasting them on long sticks over the campfire. LEFT: Sandwiches of fontina cheese on rustic bread can be roasted over the campfire; paired with mugs of tomato soup, they make a most familiar and comforting winter snack.

The Best Hot Chocolate Ever

serves 8

10 ounces best-quality bittersweet or semi-
    sweet chocolate, chopped
2 quarts milk
1 teaspoon pure vanilla extract

1. Combine chocolate and milk in a large saucepan over medium heat. Whisk until chocolate is melted and milk is very hot and frothy, about 20 minutes.
2. Remove from heat. Add vanilla; pour into a blender, filling halfway. Blend, holding lid in place (the hot liquid will expand), until frothy. Serve immediately. Blend remaining mixture.

Fire-Roasted Cheese Sandwiches

makes 8

These sandwiches can be assembled and wrapped in aluminum foil ahead of time. Roast them on a grill or directly on the embers of your campfire.

16 half-inch-thick slices bread, preferably
    rustic- or country-style
⅓ cup mustard, such as honey mustard
1 pound fontina cheese, thinly sliced

1. Spread one side of each slice of bread with mustard, and assemble eight cheese sandwiches. Wrap each in foil.
2. Place sandwiches on a medium-hot grill. Roast for about 5 to 7 minutes on each side, until the bread is golden brown and cheese is completely melted; serve immediately.

Tomato-Rice Soup

serves 8

3 tablespoons unsalted butter
1 small onion, finely chopped
1 small clove garlic, minced
2 tablespoons finely chopped fresh oregano,
    or 2 teaspoons dried, or to taste
⅔ cup uncooked converted white rice
1 teaspoon salt, plus more to taste
½ teaspoon freshly ground pepper, plus more
    to taste
3 cups homemade or low-sodium canned
    chicken stock
1 sixteen-ounce can or box of strained
    tomatoes or tomato sauce
2 cups milk

1. Melt butter over medium heat in a medium stockpot. Add onion and garlic; cook, stirring, until onion is translucent and fragrant, about 3 minutes. Add oregano, rice, salt, and pepper; continue to cook, stirring constantly, to coat the rice with butter.
2. Add stock and tomatoes or sauce; bring to a boil. Immediately reduce heat; simmer until rice is tender, about 25 minutes.
3. Stir in milk, and cook until soup is hot, about 3 to 5 minutes. Adjust seasoning to taste with salt, pepper, and oregano. Thin as needed with milk.

good thing

Ice Lanterns To make the lanterns that illuminate the pond on an early winter night, fill galvanized-steel buckets with water, then freeze them outdoors long enough to form a hard layer of ice on the top and sides. Turn each bucket upside down, and run it under hot water to dislodge the molded ice. Using a hammer and an ice pick or screwdriver, tap a wide hole through center of the inverted top. Spill out the remaining water; place a votive candle inside the molded lantern.

TOP LEFT: Mothers and daughters, gathered around the campfire's glow, sit on a circle of logs and wooden benches. TOP RIGHT: The ice lanterns, combined with a border of votive candles set in small paper bags weighted with sand, turn the frozen pond into a magical vista of fire and ice. BOTTOM, LEFT TO RIGHT: After burning calories on the ice, a happy skater samples the toasted marshmallows. Oversize oatmeal chocolate-chip cookies, each in its own wax-paper sandwich bag, are lined up in enamel pans; served this way, they can be slipped into jacket pockets and nibbled while skating. For even more energy, there are the rich and gooey banana-chocolate brownies, which get their marbled tops from swirls of a cream-cheese batter.

Oatmeal Chocolate-Chip Cookies

These cookies contain wheat germ, which can go rancid quickly; always keep it refrigerated.

1 cup light-brown sugar, packed
1 cup granulated sugar
1 cup (2 sticks) unsalted butter, at room temperature
2 large eggs, at room temperature
1 teaspoon pure vanilla extract
3 cups rolled oats
1 cup plus 2 tablespoons all-purpose flour
1 teaspoon baking soda
1 teaspoon baking powder
½ cup wheat germ
6 ounces semisweet chocolate chips
1 cup raisins
1 cup shelled walnuts, coarsely chopped

1. Heat oven to 350°. Combine light-brown sugar, granulated sugar, and butter in bowl of an electric mixer with paddle attachment. Starting on low speed and then increasing to medium, beat until mixture is creamy and fluffy, about 5 minutes. Add eggs and vanilla, scrape sides of bowl with rubber spatula, and mix to combine.
2. Combine oats, flour, baking soda, baking powder, and wheat germ in large bowl; stir to combine. Add to butter mixture; mix on low speed just to combine, 10 to 15 seconds. Remove from mixer; stir in chocolate chips, raisins, and walnuts.
3. Line baking sheets with parchment. With damp hands, shape 2 tablespoons of dough into a ball; place on a baking sheet. Repeat, spacing cookies 2 inches apart. Bake until golden brown, 15 to 17 minutes, rotating baking sheets between oven shelves halfway through the baking time. Cool on wire racks.

Banana-Split Brownies

Vegetable-oil cooking spray
6 ounces best-quality bittersweet chocolate, chopped
2 ounces best-quality unsweetened chocolate, chopped
¾ cup (1½ sticks) unsalted butter, cut into small pieces
1¼ cups sugar
4 large eggs
¾ cup plus 1 tablespoon all-purpose flour
   Pinch of salt
8 ounces cream cheese, at room temperature
1 large egg yolk
¼ cup plus 2 tablespoons confectioners' sugar
½ teaspoon pure vanilla extract
½ cup very ripe mashed banana (1 medium banana)

1. Heat oven to 350°. Spray a 9-by-13-inch baking pan with vegetable-oil spray. Bring a saucepan of water to a boil; remove from heat. Place both chocolates in a heatproof bowl; set over saucepan. Stir occasionally until completely melted.
2. Combine butter and granulated sugar in bowl of electric mixer with paddle; beat on medium low until light and fluffy, 3 to 4 minutes. Add 3 eggs; beat to combine. Scrape sides of bowl; add chocolate, ¾ cup flour, and salt. Mix until combined, 15 to 20 seconds; scrape sides of bowl once.
3. In food processor, process the cream cheese until smooth and creamy, 25 to 30 seconds. Scrape sides of the bowl; add egg yolk, confectioners' sugar, vanilla, remaining tablespoon flour, and remaining egg. Process until smooth, about 1 minute. Transfer to bowl; fold in banana.
4. Spread chocolate batter into prepared pan. With rubber spatula, make 3 trenches in batter; fill with cream-cheese batter. To marble the top, run the tip of a knife back and forth across the two batters.
5. Bake until set, about 40 minutes. Let cool on a wire rack before cutting.

Homemade Marshmallows

Marshmallows were originally made from the root of the marshmallow plant; today, corn syrup and sugar are the main ingredients. Homemade ones can be cut into any shape you like.

2½ tablespoons unflavored gelatin
1½ cups granulated sugar
1 cup light corn syrup
¼ teaspoon salt
2 tablespoons pure vanilla extract
   Confectioners' sugar, for dusting

1. Combine gelatin and ½ cup cold water in bowl of an electric mixer with whisk attachment. Let stand 30 minutes.
2. Combine granulated sugar, corn syrup, salt, and ½ cup water in a small, heavy saucepan; place over low heat, and stir until sugar has dissolved and a syrup forms. Wash down sides of pan with wet pastry brush to dissolve sugar crystals.
3. Clip on a candy thermometer; raise heat to high. Cook syrup without stirring until it reaches the firm-ball stage (244°). Immediately remove pan from heat.
4. With mixer on low speed, slowly and carefully pour syrup into the softened gelatin. Increase speed to high; beat until mixture is very thick and white and has almost tripled in volume, about 15 minutes. Add vanilla; beat to incorporate.
5. Generously dust an 8-by-12-inch glass baking pan with confectioners' sugar. Pour marshmallow mixture into pan. Dust top with confectioners' sugar; wet your hands, and pat it to smooth. Dust with confectioners' sugar again; let stand overnight, uncovered, to dry out. Turn out onto a board; cut marshmallows with a dry hot knife into 1½-inch squares, and dust with more confectioners' sugar.

GARDEN
HARVEST PARTY

CHILLED MINESTRONE

STUFFED NIÇOISE TOMATOES

CAVATELLI WITH BEETS AND SWISS CHARD

PINZIMONIO

CAESAR-SALAD SANDWICH

SUMMER SUNDAES

PECAN SHORTBREAD

OPPOSITE: Ina Garten's exuberant garden provides the freshest ingredients as well as the enchanting setting for a summer feast; Ina arranges the table and benches at the edge of her vegetable beds, bordered by Peegee hydrangeas.

The greatest joy of having a kitchen garden is to celebrate its bounty by sharing it with friends, right in the garden itself.

The best kind of vegetable garden has all the standards—tomatoes, zucchini, beans—as well as more unusual varieties—candy-cane beets, purple carrots—that are rarely found in any market. Ina Garten, who frequently entertains at her home in East Hampton, New York, plants them all, and in successive increments, so that the vegetables and herbs ripen continually throughout the summer. In April, for example, she plants a few weeks' worth of 'Genovese' and 'Purple Ruffles' basil and seven varieties of salad greens, followed by more small batches throughout May and June. Carrots, beets, and fingerling potatoes are sowed in short rows, a month at a time, so that they can be picked and served sweet and young, rather than tough and woody. Each morning, she wakes up and gazes at her garden. "It means much more to me than I ever imagined," says Ina, who owns Barefoot Contessa, a specialty-foods shop. But the keenest pleasure is to harvest whatever is ripest, and to turn it into a meal for appreciative friends. The garden dictates the menu, which is always generous and unstructured. It can be five different salads or, in this case, an appetizer of just-picked vegetables, soup, a large Caesar-salad sandwich cut into six portions, and stuffed tomatoes. The food is simple and familiar, but it is prepared and presented with flair. Pattypan squashes are hollowed out and transformed into soup bowls; zinnias bedeck the table. The smell of fresh-mown grass perfumes the air. At this party, the cohost is nature.

TOP, LEFT TO RIGHT: Ina chats with guest Brian Ramaekers. Next to the Swiss chard grow candy-cane beets, which have concentric alternating red-and-white bands, and are as tasty as they are stunning. The best extra-virgin olive oil, Parmigiano-Reggiano, and balsamic vinegar help make any meal. ABOVE LEFT: A single zinnia weights down each brightly colored napkin.

TOP LEFT: Ina and her guests, including Martha, perch at a long table covered in blue linen cut right from the bolt; only the ends needed to be hemmed. TOP RIGHT: The meal and the garden are so magnificent that the simplest of decorations is all that is required, including zinnias in jelly jars and napkins and glassware in various colors; a sprightly rosé complements a garden meal (a powerful red wine would overwhelm the delicate flavors of the food). LEFT: For the sake of visual splendor, flowers alternate with the vegetables.

To transform pattypan squashes into individual soup tureens for the chilled minestrone, carefully cut off the tops to create lids, and use a melon baller to scoop out the insides of the squashes; the charming bowls look like they were made from hand-thrown clay.

Chilled Minestrone

serves 6

Look for the smallest, most tender vegetables available. Other vegetables can be substituted to suit your taste or season.

⅓   *cup dried flageolets, rinsed and picked over; discard cracked ones*
2   *medium onions*
1   *head garlic, cut in half*
1   *three-quarter-ounce bunch marjoram*
1   *dried bay leaf*
1   *tablespoon black peppercorns*
2   *teaspoons salt, plus more to taste*
6   *large pattypan squashes, optional*
2   *tablespoons olive oil, plus more for drizzling, optional*
1   *large clove garlic, peeled*
½   *large or 1 small bulb fennel, thinly sliced and chopped*
3   *thin carrots, peeled and sliced into ¼-inch-thick circles*
1½ *quart chicken stock, preferably homemade*
1   *medium Yukon gold potato, or any other starchy cooking potato, cut into ½-inch pieces*
2   *large beefsteak tomatoes, blanched, peeled, and coarsely chopped*
1   *ear corn, kernels removed*
1   *to 2 young small zucchini, quartered and cut into ⅓-inch-thick quarter moons*
¼   *pound mixed fresh green beans, such as wax beans, string beans, and haricots verts, sliced into 1-inch pieces*
    Freshly ground pepper to taste
    Freshly squeezed lemon juice to taste
1   *recipe Basil Purée (recipe follows), optional*

1. Place flageolets in large saucepan; cover with 2 inches cold water. Slice one onion in half; add to pot. Add garlic head. Reserve 2 tablespoons marjoram leaves. Make cheesecloth sachet with remaining marjoram, bay leaf, and peppercorns; add to pot, and set over high heat. Bring to a boil, reduce heat, and simmer until beans are tender, about 45 minutes. Stir in 1 teaspoon salt 10 minutes before the beans finish cooking. Remove from heat,

and let stand in liquid to cool. Drain the beans, reserve 1 cup liquid, and discard the onion, garlic, and marjoram.

2. Trace a circle with a radius that extends two inches from the outside of the core of each pattypan squash. Cut on a diagonal to remove the core in a cone-shaped piece. Scoop with melon baller, cover with plastic, and refrigerate until needed.

3. Heat oil in stockpot over medium heat. Coarsely chop the remaining onion; add to soup pot with garlic clove. Cook until translucent, 8 minutes. Add reserved marjoram leaves, fennel, and carrots; cook, stirring, until just soft, about 15 minutes. Add stock and reserved cup bean liquid. Stir in 1 teaspoon salt and pepper to taste. Add potatoes and tomatoes; simmer 10 minutes. Add flageolets and corn; simmer until the potatoes are tender and liquid slightly stewy, about 5 minutes.

4. Raise heat to high. Stir in the zucchini and the beans. Cook about 2 minutes; remove from heat. Set pot in a bowl of ice water; stir, occasionally, until cold. Remove from ice; adjust seasoning with salt, pepper, and lemon juice. Ladle into squash or bowls; add spoonful basil purée, or drizzle of oil, to each serving.

Basil Purée

makes ⅔ cup

1   *bunch basil, leaves picked, rinsed, and patted dry*
½   *cup extra-virgin olive oil*
½   *teaspoon salt*

Combine basil, oil, and salt in a blender. Process until smooth; transfer to glass jar.

TOP: For the mini soup tureens, pick pattypan squashes with their vines on, so the vine can be used as the lid's handle. **ABOVE:** Guests enjoy themselves most while dining outside, Ina believes, when the temperature is between sixty-eight and seventy-two degrees.

Stuffed Niçoise Tomatoes

serves 6

It's fine to use leftover grilled onions in this dish. If you don't have a grill, cook onions under a hot broiler.

½   *medium red onion, sliced into ¼-inch-thick rounds*

1   *teaspoon plus 1 tablespoon olive oil*

2   *teaspoons salt, plus more to taste*
    Freshly ground pepper to taste

8   *fingerling potatoes, about ½ to ¼ ounce each, or any other small potato*

6   *twelve-ounce beefsteak tomatoes*

¼   *cup capers, rinsed of brine*

1   *four-ounce bunch arugula, coarsely chopped*

4   *teaspoons black-olive paste*

¼   *cup niçoise olives, pitted and cut in half lengthwise*

1   *teaspoon freshly squeezed lemon juice*

1   *teaspoon balsamic vinegar*

2   *six-ounce cans Italian-style tuna or solid white tuna in oil, drained*

1. Heat grill to medium hot. Brush the onions with 1 teaspoon olive oil, and sprinkle to taste with salt and pepper. Cook on the grill until soft and golden, 3 to 5 minutes per side. Remove from grill, and let cool.

2. Meanwhile, fill a medium saucepan with cold water, and add 2 teaspoons salt and potatoes. Set pot over high heat, and bring to a boil. Reduce heat, and simmer until potatoes are fork tender, 10 to 14 minutes. Drain potatoes, let stand until cool enough to handle, and rub off as much skin as possible.

3. With the point of a sharp knife, trace a circle with a one-inch radius extending from the core of each tomato. Holding the knife on the diagonal, cut along the entire circle, removing core in one cone-shaped piece; discard. Repeat process with the remaining tomatoes.

4. Slice the potatoes into long halves or quarters, depending on the size and type used. Combine onions, potatoes, capers, arugula, black-olive paste, olives, 1 tablespoon olive oil, lemon juice, and balsamic vinegar in a large mixing bowl; toss. Crumble in the tuna; toss gently. Season to taste with salt and pepper.

5. Season the cavity of each tomato with salt and pepper. Fill each tomato with tuna mixture. These will hold well at room temperature for at least 1 hour.

ABOVE: Juicy beefsteak tomatoes are stuffed with a filling of potatoes, olives, tuna, and capers; they are also seasoned with a drizzle of lemon juice and balsamic vinegar.

Cavatelli With Beets and Swiss Chard

serves 6

Because this dish tastes good at room temperature, it is perfect when entertaining a crowd. Just bake the goat cheese immediately before serving.

- *5 to 6 slices good-quality white bread*
- *2 tablespoons plus 1 teaspoon chopped fresh rosemary, plus 1 sprig*
- *½ cup extra-virgin olive oil, plus more to taste*
- *1 eight-ounce log chilled fresh goat cheese, cut into eight ½-inch-thick rounds*
- *2 pounds beets, greens removed*
- *2 tablespoons plus ½ teaspoon salt, plus more to taste*
- *½ teaspoon freshly ground pepper, plus more to taste*
- *1 pound red Swiss chard*
- *1 pound dried cavatelli or orecchiette*
- *6 to 8 cloves garlic, thinly sliced*

1. Remove and discard the crust from the bread; pulse bread in food processor into soft, small crumbs. Line a sheet pan with parchment paper. Combine the bread crumbs and 2 tablespoons rosemary in a small bowl. Pour 3 tablespoons olive oil onto a plate or a shallow bowl. Coat each round of goat cheese in olive oil, and dredge in bread-crumb mixture. Arrange the cheese on the prepared parchment-lined pan or on a large plate, and place in the refrigerator to chill until firm, at least 1 hour or overnight.

2. Heat oven to 425°. Line a baking sheet with aluminum foil. Cut the beets in half; toss with 2 tablespoons oil, 1 teaspoon salt, and ¼ teaspoon pepper. Arrange the beets in one layer on aluminum foil, cut-side down, and place the rosemary sprig on top of the beets. Cover the beets with another piece of aluminum foil, and seal the edges all around, creating a rectangular packet. Bake on the lowest shelf of oven until the beets are fork tender, about 30 minutes. Let stand until cool enough to handle. Peel the beets; cut the larger ones in half, and set aside.

3. Strip the chard leaves from the stems. Discard the stems or sauté them for later use. Rinse and drain the leaves. Do not dry them. Place the chard in a large pot over medium heat, and sprinkle with 2 teaspoons salt. Cover pot, and cook over medium heat, opening the lid only to stir, until just wilted. Remove from the heat, return to the colander, and rinse with cold water to stop them from cooking. Using your hands, gently squeeze any excess water from the chard. Coarsely chop; you should have about 2 cups. Set chard aside, but leave the pot on stove.

4. Meanwhile, fill a pasta pot with water, and set over high heat. Bring to a boil, add 1 tablespoon salt, and stir in pasta. Let cook until the pasta is al dente, about 7 to 10 minutes. Remove from heat, drain in a colander, and set aside.

5. Heat 3 tablespoons olive oil in the chard pot over medium heat. Add the garlic, and cook slowly until the garlic is just toasted, stirring often. Add the chard, remaining 1 teaspoon rosemary, ½ teaspoon salt, and ¼ teaspoon pepper, and sauté until the chard is wilted, about 3 minutes. Add the pasta, toss, and cook just until hot. Adjust the seasoning to taste with the olive oil, salt, and pepper, and transfer the pasta to a large serving platter. Arrange the beets over the pasta.

6. Bake the cheese in the oven until very soft to the touch, heated through, and golden brown, 6 to 7 minutes. Remove from oven, arrange warm cheese around platter of pasta, and serve immediately.

TOP: Beets are roasted with rosemary and olive oil, and mixed with sautéed Swiss chard, cavatelli, and baked goat cheese. **ABOVE:** The beets are just one of the heirloom vegetables that Ina cultivates; others include purple carrots, haricots verts, and fingerling potatoes.

Pinzimonio

serves **6** to **8**

It is essential to use the best-quality extra-virgin olive oil and coarse sea salt for this Italian appetizer. Virtually any summer vegetable will work; if using vegetables from your garden, try to pick them, or allow your guests to pick their own, as close to serving time as possible.

6 *to 8 large red cabbage leaves, wiped of*
grit with a damp cloth

2 *bunches young carrots, trimmed, peeled,*
and cut in half lengthwise

2 *bunches young purple carrots, trimmed,*
scrubbed, and cut in half lengthwise

6 *large cucumbers, cut into spears*

2 *green bell peppers, ribs and seeds removed,*
cut into ½-inch strips
Best-quality extra-virgin olive oil
Coarse sea salt

Place the cabbage leaves on a wooden board or serving plate. Arrange the vegetables on each leaf, using the cabbage leaves to cradle the vegetables. Serve with olive oil and salt for dipping.

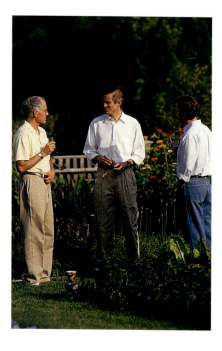

ABOVE: The garden is luminous at night, lit with dozens of votives. LEFT: At a garden party, conversation flows from tomatoes to politics and back again. OPPOSITE, TOP AND BOTTOM: A Caesar-salad sandwich. The pinzimonio can be served as an appetizer, then sampled throughout the meal.

Caesar-Salad Sandwich

serves 6

Choose a rectangular rustic loaf that's long but not too thick, with crisp crust and a soft interior.

1 pint cherry tomatoes, sliced in half lengthwise
½ cup plus 3 tablespoons extra-virgin olive oil
1 tablespoon balsamic vinegar
¼ teaspoon salt
¼ teaspoon freshly ground pepper, plus more to taste
1 clove garlic, pressed in garlic press or smashed to a paste
Juice of 2 lemons (about 4 tablespoons)
3 anchovies, rinsed and chopped
½ teaspoon Dijon mustard
1 twelve-to-sixteen-ounce oblong loaf rustic bread
1 head romaine lettuce (about 1¼ pounds), limp outer leaves discarded, inner leaves separated and left whole
2 ounces Parmigiano-Reggiano, shaved as thinly as possible

1. Heat oven to 250°. Line a baking sheet with parchment. Place tomatoes in mixing bowl with 3 tablespoons olive oil, 1 tablespoon vinegar, ½ teaspoon salt, and ⅛ teaspoon pepper; toss to coat. Spread tomatoes, cut-side up, on prepared pan. Bake until starting to wrinkle but still juicy, about 1 hour. Remove from oven; set aside to cool. Raise oven temperature to 375°.

2. In jar with lid, combine garlic, lemon juice, anchovies, ½ cup olive oil, ¼ teaspoon salt, ⅛ teaspoon pepper, and ½ teaspoon mustard. Tighten lid, and shake.

3. Slice the loaf of bread open lengthwise, leaving a hinge on one side; remove most of the crumb. Toast in the oven until golden, about 6 minutes.

4. Drizzle small amount of dressing over bread; toss the remaining dressing with romaine, half the cheese, and pepper to taste. Arrange romaine on bottom half of bread, sprinkle tomatoes and cheese over romaine; close sandwich. Slice crosswise into six pieces; serve.

good thing

Outdoor Votives At a garden party that goes from afternoon into darkness, there can never be enough candles to light the table, the garden paths, the steps to the house, and the front gate. Brush insides and top rims of miniature terra cotta pots with silver acrylic paint. When dry, place a votive candle inside; the silver coating will reflect the flame. To make these hanging votives, secure two crossed slings of wire to jelly jars with colored rubber bands; twist the four strands of wire together to form the hooks.

Summer Sundaes

serves 6

Make the caramel, slice the fruit, and toast the pecans; then let your guests make their own sundaes, as they like.

> 2   *cups sugar*
> ½   *pint heavy cream*
> 1   *vanilla bean, split*
> 2   *pints premium-quality sorbet in two flavors, such as raspberry and mango*
> 1   *pint premium-quality ice cream, such as vanilla*
> 2   *ripe peaches, sliced*
> 2   *ripe plums, sliced*
> ½   *pint raspberries*
> ½   *pint blueberries*
> ½   *pint strawberries, hulled*
> 1   *pint figs, cut in half*
> 1   *cup pecan halves, toasted*

1. Combine sugar and ¼ cup water in a medium-sized heavy-bottomed saucepan. Cook over medium-low heat until sugar is dissolved. Cover pan; bring to a boil. Leave cover on until condensation washes down insides of pan. If syrup crystallizes, let it crystallize completely, and push it around bottom of saucepan with the back of a wooden spoon until it melts again. Raise heat to medium high; cook, swirling pan occasionally, until the sugar turns medium-dark amber. Carefully add the cream, standing back in case the sugar boils over, and scrape in the vanilla seeds. Stir until cream is incorporated, and remove from heat. Let cool; transfer to a glass jar, bottle, or bowl for storing and serving.
2. Scoop sorbets and ice cream into serving dishes, drizzle with caramel, and spoon fruit over sauce. Serve, garnished with the toasted pecans.

Pecan Shortbread

makes about 1½ dozen

This cookie is always the first to sell out at the Barefoot Contessa, Ina Garten's gourmet store in East Hampton, New York.

> 1   *cup unsalted butter, room temperature*
> ½   *cup sugar, plus 2 tablespoons for sprinkling*
> ½   *teaspoon pure vanilla extract*
> 1¾   *cups all-purpose flour*
>   *Pinch salt*
> 2¼   *ounces whole pecan halves, toasted*
> 2   *drops almond extract*

1. Cream together butter, ½ cup sugar, and vanilla in bowl of electric mixer, until mixture is light in color, 3 to 4 minutes.
2. Add flour, salt, pecans, and almond extract; mix until combined and the pecans start to break up.
3. Wrap dough in plastic wrap, and place in refrigerator at least 1 hour or overnight. On a lightly floured surface, roll out dough to a ¼-inch thickness. Using 2½-inch-diameter fluted cookie cutters, cut the cookies, and place them on parchment-lined baking sheet. Return cookies to refrigerator 1 hour more.
4. Heat oven to 325°. Sprinkle cookies with the remaining sugar, and bake until lightly browned, 15 to 20 minutes. Transfer to a wire rack, and let cool.

Let your guests compose their own sundaes of ice cream and sorbets, sliced summer fruit and berries, toasted pecans, and a drizzle of homemade caramel; pecan shortbread completes the treat.

SOUL-FOOD BRUNCH

SOUTHERN-COMFORT PUNCH

HUSH PUPPIES

FRIED OKRA

SHRIMP-AND-CRAB GUMBO

MESS O'GREENS

MACARONI AND CHEESE

DIRTY RICE

BUTTERMILK BISCUITS

SWEET-POTATO BUTTER

SWEET-POTATO TARTLETS

VANILLA TEA CAKE

PEANUT BRITTLE

OPPOSITE: Sheila Bridges, far left, hosts a leisurely Sunday brunch in her Manhattan apartment, clearing space so guests can mingle, draw chairs into intimate groupings, and pass Teddy Alexander, her friends' toddler, from lap to lap.

A mix of updated soul food, Cajun specialties, and Southern sweets encourages a long, informal get-together in Harlem.

When Sheila Bridges, an interior designer in Manhattan, moved to her apartment, she was drawn not only by the space and light, but also by the neighborhood. "It's in Harlem, a place that for me, an African-American, has a rich cultural history," she says. When she hosts a brunch for friends and their little children, Bridges encourages the sharing of talents: One guest might read from a book she's writing; another might play a new song. It is Sunday afternoon, and no one is in a hurry. At a buffet, a father can excuse himself to tend to a child without feeling he has disrupted the party's rhythm, or the child can wander around willy-nilly. The food Bridges serves is a link to history. She starts out with the traditional soul-food dishes African-Americans created in the rural South, many of which are now reserved mainly for holidays and family gatherings. But Bridges makes the dishes lighter: She cooks greens with smoked turkey wings rather than with ham hocks, and uses turkey sausage, not andouille, in the gumbo. The simply set table, which is in harmony with the living room, lends elegance to the food. Even macaroni and cheese, made with cheddar, Parmesan, and goat cheeses and presented in a fluted china dish, no longer seems so humble. Friends refill their plates at will, and talk continues through the afternoon, about the past and plans for the future.

TOP, LEFT TO RIGHT: Dressing up: Pale-pink roses are massed in an amber glass bowl. Coffee is served in gold-rimmed porcelain. Fruit placed in a voluptuous glass jar is an edible alternative to another arrangement of flowers. ABOVE LEFT: Bridges sets out spoons and serving dishes before filling them with food, in order to see the layout of the buffet and to make the table more visually engaging when guests arrive. OPPOSITE: By alternating dishes set flat on the table with those that are raised, Bridges creates a rhythmic pattern; the three pale linen runners complement the room's colors and serving pieces.

ABOVE: To welcome her guests, Bridges offers Southern-Comfort punch, layered with paper-thin slices of lemons and oranges; she also brings out plates of fried okra and hush puppies spiked with jalapeños as appetizers. OPPOSITE: Gumbo is a mainstay of Creole cuisine; this version gets so much flavor from turkey sausage, shrimp, and peppers that nobody misses the more traditional pork sausage.

Southern-Comfort Punch

serves 12 to 20

This recipe is one of Sheila Bridges' favorites; every time she makes it, she says, it gets a little bit better.

> 6 *lemons*
> 4 *navel oranges*
> 2 *six-ounce cans frozen lemonade concentrate*
> 1 *six-ounce can frozen orange juice concentrate*
> 2 *liters Sprite*
> 1 *liter Southern Comfort*

1. Line 2 baking sheets with plastic wrap, and set aside. Slice lemons into rounds as thin as possible. Arrange lemon slices in layers on one prepared baking sheet. Repeat with oranges; layer on second baking sheet. Place in the freezer for 2 to 2½ hours, or until fruit slices are frozen.
2. Just before serving, open the cans of frozen lemonade and orange juice, and place the frozen concentrates, whole, in a large punch bowl. Add the Sprite, Southern Comfort, and several handfuls of ice cubes. Remove frozen fruit slices from freezer; arrange over top of punch. Serve.

Hush Puppies

makes about 38

> 4 *cups peanut oil*
> 1½ *cups all-purpose flour*
> ¼ *cup yellow cornmeal*
> 2 *teaspoons baking powder*
> 1½ *teaspoons baking soda*
> 1 *teaspoon salt*
> ⅛ *teaspoon cayenne pepper*
> 2 *tablespoons minced jalapeño pepper*
> 2 *large eggs*
> 1 *cup buttermilk*

1. Heat oil in a 2½-quart saucepan over medium heat until it reaches 375° on an instant-read thermometer.
2. Meanwhile, whisk together flour, cornmeal, baking powder, baking soda, salt, and cayenne in bowl. Mix in the jalapeño.
3. In another bowl, whisk together eggs and buttermilk. Add to flour mixture; stir to combine. Mixture will be slightly lumpy.
4. Drop heaping teaspoons of batter into hot oil without crowding. Fry until golden brown, turning once or twice, 2 to 3 minutes. Use slotted spoon to transfer to paper towel to drain. Serve immediately.

Fried Okra

serves 10 to 12

> 5 *cups vegetable shortening*
> 4 *large eggs*
> 2 *tablespoons milk*
> 2 *cups all-purpose flour*
> 2 *cups cornmeal*
> 1½ *teaspoons salt*
> ½ *teaspoon freshly ground pepper*
> 1 *pound fresh okra, stems trimmed*

1. Melt shortening in a 12-inch cast-iron skillet over medium heat until a frying thermometer registers 375°.
2. Meanwhile, whisk together eggs and milk in a bowl. Place flour, cornmeal, salt, and pepper in another bowl; whisk to combine.
3. Place eight pieces of okra in egg mixture to coat, then dredge in flour mixture. Fry until golden brown, turning as necessary, 3 to 4 minutes. Drain fried okra on paper towels. Repeat coating-and-frying process; serve warm.

Shrimp-and-Crab Gumbo

serves 10 to 12

"Gumbo" comes from the Bantu word for okra, a key ingredient in this Creole stew.

- 2 pounds medium shrimp
- 8 ounces turkey sausage, casing removed
- 2 medium onions, minced
- 2 medium green bell peppers, cored and seeded, cut into ¼-inch dice
- 1 pound okra, cut crosswise into quarters
- 2 jalapeño peppers, ribs and seeds removed, minced
- ¼ teaspoon gumbo filé (powdered sassafras leaves; available in supermarkets)
- 1½ teaspoons salt
- ½ teaspoon freshly ground pepper
- 2 teaspoons finely chopped fresh thyme
- ¾ cup Dark Roux (recipe follows)
- 6 cups Shrimp Stock (recipe follows)
- ¾ cup chopped canned peeled tomatoes
- 6 blue crabs (6 to 8 ounces each), optional
- 1 pound jumbo lump crabmeat, picked over for shells
- 3 tablespoons chopped flat-leaf parsley

1. Shell and devein shrimp, leaving tail sections intact; reserve shells for stock. Break sausage into ½-inch pieces; in a skillet, cook over medium heat until all the fat has been rendered, about 8 minutes. Mix in onions, green peppers, okra, jalapeño, and filé. Cook until onions have softened, about 10 minutes. Add salt, pepper, and thyme. Reduce heat to low; cook 5 minutes more. Set aside.

2. Melt Dark Roux over medium heat in stockpot; heat Shrimp Stock in medium saucepan over high heat. Gradually pour hot stock over roux, whisking to combine well. Cook over medium-low heat until the mixture thickens, 6 to 8 minutes. Reduce heat to low; add reserved sausage-and-vegetable mixture and tomatoes. Stir gumbo well; let cook for 1 hour.

3. If using whole crabs, cut them in half lengthwise, and add to gumbo. Cook 2 to 3 minutes. Add shrimp, and cook 3 to 4 minutes, or until opaque. Add crabmeat and parsley; cook 2 to 4 minutes. Season to taste. Serve hot over Dirty Rice.

Dark Roux

makes ¾ cup

This can also be made on the stovetop, though it tends to burn more easily: In step two, cook over medium heat, stirring occasionally, until dark brown, forty-five to sixty minutes.

- ½ cup vegetable shortening
- ¾ cups all-purpose flour

1. Place rack in center of oven. Heat oven to 325°. Melt shortening in a 10-inch cast-iron skillet over medium-low heat. Gradually sift flour over shortening; whisk to combine. The mixture will be thick and pasty. Continue to whisk until light brown, 10 to 12 minutes.

2. Transfer skillet to oven; let roux cook until very dark brown, 3 to 3½ hours, whisking every 45 minutes (whisk every 30 minutes if pan is not cast iron). The roux can be kept, refrigerated, for up to a week before using.

Shrimp Stock

makes about 6 cups

- 1 tablespoon vegetable shortening
- 1 medium onion, peeled, cut into eighths
- 1 carrot, peeled, cut into ½-inch pieces
- 1 celery stalk, cut into ½-inch pieces
- 2 bay leaves
- 2 quarter-inch-thick slices lemon
- 1 jalapeño pepper, cut in half lengthwise
- 6 sprigs fresh flat-leaf parsley
- 2 sprigs fresh thyme
- 1 teaspoon salt
- 1 teaspoon black peppercorns
  Shells from 2 pounds of shrimp

Melt the shortening in a stockpot over medium heat. Add all remaining ingredients. Cook, stirring frequently, about 10 minutes. Add 3 quarts water; cover. Bring to a boil over high heat. Reduce heat to low; simmer, uncovered, for 1 hour. Strain through a sieve; discard solids.

A sampling from Bridges' buffet table includes collard greens, a biscuit with sweet-potato butter, shrimp-and-crab gumbo over dirty rice, and macaroni and cheese; the delicate porcelain contrasts with the more hearty and homey food.

Mess o' Greens

serves 10 to 12

2 tablespoons olive oil

5 medium leeks, white and light-green
parts only, cut into ¼-inch rounds

2 cloves garlic, peeled

1 teaspoon red-pepper flakes

1 smoked turkey wing (4 to 6 ounces), cut
into 3-inch pieces

3 pounds greens, such as collard, mustard,
turnip, and kale, washed thoroughly,
trimmed, and torn into pieces

¼ cup dry white wine

¾ teaspoon salt

¼ teaspoon freshly ground black pepper

1. Heat olive oil in a large stockpot or casserole over medium-high heat until hot, 2 to 3 minutes. Add leeks and garlic; stir to coat. Cook, stirring, until leeks are softened but not brown, about 3 minutes. Add red-pepper flakes, pieces of smoked turkey wing, and greens; if necessary, add the greens in several batches.
2. Add wine; cover. Steam greens, turning occasionally, 8 to 10 minutes. Uncover, add salt and pepper, and cook, tossing occasionally, 3 minutes. Discard turkey and garlic; serve.

Macaroni and Cheese

serves 10 to 12

Choose sharp, full-flavored cheeses to give this dish the most impact.

8 tablespoons (1 stick) plus 1 tablespoon
unsalted butter, plus more for casserole

4 cups uncooked elbow macaroni

5 cups milk

½ cup plus 1 tablespoon all-purpose flour

1 teaspoon salt

¼ teaspoon freshly ground pepper

¼ teaspoon cayenne pepper

2 cups grated sharp yellow cheddar

2 cups grated sharp white cheddar

1 cup freshly grated Parmesan

20 scallions, white and light-green parts
only, thinly sliced

5 ounces fresh goat cheese

1. Heat oven to 375°. Lightly butter a 2-quart casserole. Set aside. Cook the macaroni in a large pot of boiling water according to package instructions. Drain, rinse with cool water to stop the cooking, and set aside.
2. Warm the milk in medium saucepan over medium-low heat. Melt the butter in large, heavy pot over medium heat. Gradually whisk in flour; cook for 2 minutes, or until mixture is thick and smooth. Whisking constantly, gradually add warm milk. Cook over medium-low heat 8 to 10 minutes, whisking occasionally. Remove the white sauce from heat; add the salt, pepper, and cayenne.
3. In a bowl, combine ¼ cup each yellow and white cheddars and ¼ cup Parmesan; set aside. Reserve 1 tablespoon scallions. Add remaining yellow and white cheddars and ¾ cup Parmesan to the warm white sauce. Stir well. Stir in the remaining scallions, then macaroni. Add goat cheese in 1-inch pieces; fold gently to combine.
4. Transfer the mixture to casserole, and top with reserved scallions and cheeses. Bake until golden brown and bubbling, 30 to 35 minutes.

don't forget

• One end of every buffet table needs to be set with more than enough napkins and utensils for all your guests. Rather than letting flatware spread over the limited surface of your table, bundle each place setting (or knife and fork, if they suffice) in a napkin. Guests, as they balance their filled plates and glasses, will find it much easier to retrieve what they need. Below, linen napkins are rolled around the cutlery, tied with fresh spears of lily grass (available from florists), and offered in a graceful tole basket set on a side table. Any pretty bowl, box, cachepot, or other container in the right size will work just as well. Try tying napkins with bows of ribbon, silk cord, seam binding, or rickrack.

Dirty Rice

serves 10 to 12

- 1½ cups long-grain rice
- 2½ teaspoons salt
- 1 tablespoon unsalted butter
- 3 tablespoons vegetable oil
- 1 medium red onion, finely chopped
- 2 cloves garlic, peeled, finely chopped
- ½ pound chicken livers, cleaned and finely chopped
- 2 scallions, trimmed, white and green parts cut crosswise into ⅛-inch pieces
- 2 celery stalks, including leafy greens, finely chopped
- ¼ cup finely chopped green bell pepper
- ½ cup finely chopped red bell pepper
- 2 tablespoons chopped flat-leaf parsley
- 2 tablespoons chopped fresh oregano, or 2 teaspoons dried
- 1 jalapeño pepper, seeds and ribs removed, finely chopped
- ½ teaspoon freshly ground pepper

1. Bring 3 cups water to a boil in sauce-pan. Stir in the rice, 1 teaspoon salt, and butter. Cover, reduce heat to low, and cook 15 to 17 minutes, until the water is absorbed. Set aside.

2. Heat the oil in a cast-iron skillet over medium-high heat. Add onion and garlic; reduce heat to medium. Cook, stirring occasionally, until brown, about 10 minutes. Add chicken livers; cook, stirring constantly, 5 minutes. Add rice and all remaining ingredients. Cook, tossing and stirring, until hot, 2 to 3 minutes.

Buttermilk Biscuits

makes 36

- 5 cups all-purpose flour
- 1 teaspoon baking soda
- 1 tablespoon baking powder
- 2 teaspoons salt
- 2½ tablespoons sugar
- 2 packages (¼ ounce) active dry yeast
- 1 cup (2 sticks) unsalted butter, cut into small pieces, plus 4 tablespoons unsalted butter, melted and cooled
- 2 cups buttermilk

1. Heat oven to 450°. Line 3 baking sheets with parchment. Sift together flour, baking soda, baking powder, salt, and sugar.

2. Place ¼ cup warm water (about 110°) in a small bowl; sprinkle with yeast; let stand 5 minutes. Use a pastry cutter to blend the 1 cup of butter into the flour mixture until it resembles coarse meal. Stir in yeast mixture and buttermilk. Turn onto a floured surface, and knead until smooth, 2 to 3 minutes.

3. Roll dough to a thickness of ¼ inch. Cut out 2½-inch rounds; place 2 inches apart on baking sheet. Knead dough scraps lightly; continue cutting rounds, using all dough. Brush edges with melted butter, fold rounds in half, and press edges to seal. Brush tops with butter. Place 2 baking sheets in the oven; leave third sheet at room temperature. Bake 6 minutes; rotate baking sheets between oven racks; bake until lightly golden, 5 to 6 minutes more. Bake third sheet on center rack for 8 to 10 minutes. Serve warm.

Sweet-Potato Butter

makes 2 cups

2 *pounds sweet potatoes (about 5)*

6 *tablespoons unsalted butter*

1 *medium shallot, peeled and thinly sliced*

¼ *cup cider vinegar*

1½ *teaspoons finely grated fresh ginger*

2½ *teaspoons dry mustard*

½ *teaspoon cayenne pepper*

½ *teaspoon salt*

⅛ *teaspoon freshly ground pepper*

1. Heat oven to 400°. Prick the sweet potatoes. Place on baking sheet, and cook about 40 minutes, or until soft. Let cool.

2. Peel sweet potatoes, cut into chunks, and set aside. Melt 2 tablespoons butter in an 8-inch skillet over medium heat. Reduce the heat to medium low, and add shallots; cook, stirring occasionally, until caramelized, 6 to 8 minutes. Add vinegar; cook 2 minutes. Stir in ginger, mustard, cayenne, salt, and pepper. Cook over low heat, 2 to 3 minutes.

3. Place potatoes in a food processor; add shallot mixture; process until smooth. Transfer mixture to a heavy saucepan. Over low heat, cook 1 hour, stirring often, until mixture takes on a deep, rich color. Cool completely.

4. Transfer mixture to an electric-mixer bowl. Add the remaining 4 tablespoons butter in small pieces; whip until fluffy, and serve with biscuits.

LEFT: The casual atmosphere of Bridges' buffet makes children as welcome as adults. BELOW: Butter-milk biscuits are piled high in a napkin-lined white porcelain fruit compote; the accompanying sweet-potato butter is in a bowl nearby.

Sweet-Potato Tartlets

makes 12

For the filling:

- 2 *small sweet potatoes (1 pound total)*
- 1 *large egg, lightly beaten, at room temperature*
- ¼ *cup heavy cream*
- 2 *tablespoons unsulfured molasses*
- 1 *teaspoon pure vanilla extract*
- ¼ *cup packed light-brown sugar*
- ⅛ *teaspoon salt*
- ¼ *teaspoon ground ginger*
- ¼ *teaspoon ground cinnamon*
  Pinch ground cloves
  Pinch allspice

For the praline topping and crust:

- 1¼ *cups whole pecans*
- 1 *cup granulated sugar*
- 10 *tablespoons unsalted butter, chilled, cut into small pieces*
- ¾ *cup light-brown sugar*
- 1¼ *cups plus 2 tablespoons all-purpose flour*
- ½ *teaspoon salt*
- ¼ *teaspoon cinnamon*

1. To make the filling: Heat oven to 400°. Prick potatoes. Place on baking sheet; bake about 40 minutes, or until soft. When cool enough to handle, peel and mash.

2. Transfer mashed potatoes to bowl of an electric mixer; beat on low speed for 1 minute. Whisk together egg, cream, molasses, and vanilla. Add to potatoes; mix on low speed, 1 to 2 minutes. Mix in the remaining filling ingredients. Let stand until crusts are ready.

3. To make topping and crust: Begin by making pecan praline. Place ½ cup pecans on a large parchment-lined baking sheet. In a small, heavy saucepan, combine granulated sugar and 2 tablespoons water. Cook over low heat until the sugar dissolves. Cover, and bring to a boil. Leave cover on until condensation washes down insides of pan. Uncover, adjust heat to medium, and cook, swirling pan occasionally, until sugar turns amber. Pour caramel over pecans; let cool about 1 hour. Chop praline into small pieces.

4. Meanwhile, heat oven to 350°. On a rimmed baking sheet, toast the remaining ¾ cup pecans for about 7 minutes, turning once. Let cool completely. Transfer to a food processor, and process to fine powder; add butter, brown sugar, flour, salt, and cinnamon. Pulse until well combined.

5. Set aside ½ cup of mixture to use for topping. Divide rest among 3-inch tart tins; press into tins. Refrigerate on a baking sheet for 30 minutes. Poke crusts with a fork, and bake 5 minutes.

6. Place tart tins on a work surface, and spoon sweet-potato filling into each. Crumble reserved topping into small pieces between your fingers; mix in half the chopped pecan praline. Sprinkle this topping over the sweet-potato filling, carefully avoiding edges of the crust. Place tarts on a baking sheet, transfer to oven, and bake for 25 to 35 minutes, until the tarts are puffed and golden brown. Transfer to a wire rack to cool 15 to 20 minutes. Unmold, and let cool to room temperature. Sprinkle remaining pecan praline over tarts; serve.

Vanilla Tea Cake

serves 10 to 12

- 2 *cups cake flour plus more for pan*
- ½ *teaspoon salt*
- 1 *teaspoon baking powder*
- ½ *pound (2 sticks) unsalted butter, at room temperature, plus more for pan*
- 1½ *cups sugar*
- 5 *large eggs*
- 2 *teaspoons pure vanilla extract*

1. Grease and flour a 10-by-5-by-3-inch loaf pan. Line bottom with parchment. With rack in center, heat oven to 325°. Place baking sheet on rack to heat. Sift together flour, salt, and baking powder.

2. In bowl of electric mixer with paddle attachment, beat the butter on medium speed until light and fluffy, 3 to 4 minutes. Gradually add sugar; beat until creamy. Beat in eggs one at a time. Add vanilla; beat until creamy.

3. With mixer on lowest speed, gradually add flour mixture. Mix until incorporated.

4. Scrape batter into prepared pan; tap on countertop to settle. Place pan on baking sheet in oven. Bake 1 hour to 1 hour and 15 minutes, until cake is golden on top and a tester inserted into center comes out clean.

5. Let pan cool on a rack for 1 hour. Slide knife around cake to loosen. Invert pan to remove cake, then place upright on rack. When completely cool, wrap cake tightly in plastic wrap, and let stand 24 hours before serving.

Peanut Brittle

serves 10 to 12

- *Vegetable-oil cooking spray*
- 3 *cups sugar*
- 1 *cup light corn syrup*
- 4½ *cups salted, roasted peanuts, skinned*
- 2 *teaspoons baking soda*
- 4 *tablespoons unsalted butter*
- 2 *teaspoons pure vanilla extract*

1. Coat two 17-by-12-by-1-inch baking pans with vegetable-oil spray. In a heavy 5-quart saucepan, combine sugar, corn syrup, and ½ cup water. Clip on a candy thermometer. Stirring constantly with a wooden spoon, bring mixture to a boil over high heat; stop stirring. Wash down sides of pan with a wet pastry brush to remove sugar crystals. Reduce heat to medium; boil until temperature reaches 230° (thread stage), 5 to 10 minutes.

2. Add peanuts; stir constantly until the mixture reaches 300° (hard-crack stage), about 25 minutes. Remove from heat, and quickly add baking soda, butter, and vanilla. Stir with wooden spoon just until butter melts. Pour half the mixture down the center of each pan. Mixture will be very foamy. Use a metal spatula to spread mixture while warm. Let cool at least 1 hour. Turn out of pan, and break into shards. Brittle may be kept in an airtight container for several weeks.

ABOVE: The second buffet table, just for desserts: vanilla tea cake served with fresh berries and whipped cream, homemade peanut brittle, and sweet-potato tartlets, which have ground pecans in the crust and more pecans in the praline topping. Spoons are ready in a green glass, next to the plates.

FAMILY COUNTRY
PICNIC

CINNAMON-PECAN STICKY BUNS

DIG-DEEP LAYERED SUMMER SALAD

COTTAGE CHEESE-DILL SKILLET BREAD

MACARONI-AND-POTATO SALAD

BARBECUED CHICKEN BREASTS WITH

SPICY PEACH GLAZE

SWEET CORN

CHERRY LEMONADE

SOUR-CHERRY AND PEACH-RASPBERRY PIES

OPPOSITE: On a midwestern farm, a massive red barn is the backdrop for a three-generation family picnic; the makeshift barn-door-and-sawhorse table is ringed by an assortment of chairs that have seen many summer gatherings.

At the peak of summer, an all-day picnic brings together family and friends under a vast, brilliant blue prairie sky.

Summer is the season when all rules ought to be reconsidered. Three quick meals a day might make sense the rest of the year, when there are school buses to catch and sports practices to work around. But in summer? Why rush? Call it lunch, call it dinner, let it start at noon and stretch all the way into evening. Everyone, from newborns to grandparents to great-grandparents to kissing cousins, is welcome. Invitations can be issued spontaneously, even the day before—the moment you can reasonably expect the weather will be tolerable (no more than 85° in the shade). The food should be simple and fresh and planned to taste best room-temperature. And because a picnic is traditionally a potluck meal, you can ask people to bring whatever they want. One guest might offer to be the designated pie maker; another, who doesn't want to cook, might bring a sampling of her pickled string beans and cucumbers made the year before. Instead of food, someone might bring flowers or, if needed, extra chairs. Since you don't want to be tied down with hours of preparation, you can get a head start, and pace yourself: Layer the dig-deep salad and grill chicken breasts with a peach glaze the night before (both dishes are even more flavorful after spending the night in the refrigerator); bake the sticky buns in the cool of the morning. The charm of a picnic is its unabashed informality: The only dress code is bare feet and smiles. Children can shuck the corn, pick flowers for arrangements, or help set the table with a simple cotton cloth. Odds are good that, by the end of the day, all pies will have been properly polished off.

TOP, LEFT TO RIGHT: Lemonade, spiked with cherry juice, is refreshing and colorful. A metal toolbox is a convenient carrying case for flatware. Day-old corn simmered in milk and water gains sweetness. ABOVE LEFT: By the time the sun sets, only the chairs, tablecloth, and lantern have to be put away.

CLOCKWISE, FROM TOP LEFT: Hay bales will feed the animals in winter. Built as a summer kitchen, this one-room clapboard cottage makes an excellent weekend hideaway. Chairs, hung from nails, Shaker-style, await the next picnic. Use lots of ice and rock salt to help ice cream freeze before the ice-cream churners tire. The pie bearer will be a welcome arrival. Every picnic need, including a vase of wildflowers, is carried in a large basket and secured by bungee cords. A tire swing can lift anyone's mood. The cornfield with its sweet, ripe corn, ready for picking.

Cinnamon-Pecan Sticky Buns

makes 12

These sticky buns have to be started the night before, but they're so delicious, they're worth the extra time.

2   packages active dry yeast (1 tablespoon plus 1 teaspoon)
1   cup plus 2 tablespoons warm milk (about 110°)
6   cups all-purpose flour
⅓   cup granulated sugar
2   teaspoons salt
4   large eggs
1   pound (4 sticks) unsalted butter, room temperature, cut up, plus more for the pan
3⅓   cups pecan halves
2¼   cups light corn syrup
1½   cups packed dark-brown sugar
½   cup plus 3 tablespoons sour cream
1   tablespoon cinnamon

1. In a small bowl, combine the yeast and the milk. Let stand until the yeast is creamy, about 10 minutes. In the bowl of an electric mixer, combine the flour, granulated sugar, and salt. Add the yeast mixture and eggs; mix on low speed until completely combined, about 3 minutes.

2. Increase the speed to high, and add the butter, several pieces at a time. When all the butter has been added, continue mixing dough until smooth and shiny, 8 to 10 minutes. Transfer the dough to a parchment-lined 13-by-18-inch baking pan, and use your hands to spread the dough out to fit the pan. Cover the pan with plastic wrap, and place in the refrigerator to chill overnight.

3. Heat the oven to 350°. Generously butter one 12-cup muffin pan or two 6-cup, 7-ounce capacity pans. Chop 2 cups pecans, and break the remaining 1⅓ cups pecans in half lengthwise, keeping the two types separate. Pour 3 tablespoons corn syrup into each muffin cup, and add about 1 tablespoon of brown sugar to each muffin cup. Add about 2 table-spoons of the halved pecans to each

muffin cup; set the filled muffin pan aside.

4. Remove the dough from refrigerator, and let stand at room temperature until slightly softened, about 15 minutes. Roll out the dough lengthwise, ¼ inch thick by 15 inches long by 20 inches wide. Using a spatula, spread the sour cream over the surface of the dough, leaving a ½-inch border. Dust the sour cream with cinnamon; sprinkle with ⅔ cup brown sugar. Cover brown sugar with chopped pecans, and roll dough up lengthwise to form roll 18 inches long by 3 inches in diameter.

5. Using a sharp knife, slice dough into 1½-inch-thick slices, and place in the prepared pan or pans, either cut-side down, until every cup is filled. Cover buns with parchment paper, and let rise in a warm place until they are ½ inch above cups, 20 to 30 minutes. Transfer sticky buns to the oven, placing a cookie sheet on the rack below to catch any drips. Rotate the pans between the shelves to ensure even baking, until the buns are dark golden brown, about 40 minutes.

6. Remove the pans from the oven, and immediately turn the buns out onto a second, parchment-covered cookie sheet. Replace any pecan halves that fell off the buns when turning them out. Place the cookie sheet on a wire rack to cool.

TOP: Homemade cinnamon sticky buns and freshly picked blackberries, both classic picnic fare, may well disappear before the meal—or be saved for dessert. **ABOVE:** The dig-deep salad, made the day before and refrigerated so that the flavors blend, includes wheat berries, celery, dried cherries, cabbage, and blue cheese; a glass bowl shows off its colorful layers.

Dig-Deep Layered Summer Salad

serves 8 to 10

This layered salad has a variety of tastes and textures all the way through. Dig deep to the bottom to get the best mix.

- 2 cups hard wheat berries (pearl barley can be substituted)
- 6 tablespoons freshly squeezed lemon juice (about 2 lemons)
- ¼ cup white-wine vinegar
- 4 teaspoons Dijon mustard
- 1½ teaspoons salt
- ¼ teaspoon freshly ground pepper
- 1 tablespoon sugar
- ½ teaspoon celery seed
- 1 cup olive oil
- ¼ bunch celery, strings removed, sliced thinly on the diagonal (about 2¼ cups)
- 1½ cups dried tart cherries
- 10 ounces Maytag blue cheese, crumbled (2⅓ cups)
- 1 small head green cabbage, thinly shredded (about 5 cups)
- 5 large carrots, peeled and grated (about 5 cups)

1. Place wheat berries in a small stockpot, and add 2 quarts water. Cover, and bring to a boil. Reduce heat to low, and simmer the berries until tender, about 40 minutes. Drain in a colander, and transfer to a large glass serving bowl.

2. In a medium bowl, whisk together the lemon juice, vinegar, mustard, salt, pepper, sugar, and celery seed. In a slow, steady stream, whisk in the olive oil until completely combined. Drizzle 2 tablespoons dressing over the wheat berries.

3. Arrange the celery slices over wheat berries, and drizzle with 2 tablespoons dressing. Cover the celery with cherries, and drizzle with 2 tablespoons dressing.

4. Crumble half the blue cheese over the top of the cherries, and drizzle with 2 tablespoons dressing.

5. In a medium bowl, toss together the shredded cabbage and 3 tablespoons dressing; layer cabbage over blue cheese. Layer carrots over cabbage, and drizzle with 2 tablespoons dressing. Crumble remaining blue cheese over carrots, and drizzle with remaining dressing. Cover the salad, and transfer to the refrigerator for 24 hours to allow flavors to develop. Serve salad at room temperature.

Cottage Cheese-Dill Skillet Bread

serves 8

Right before serving, brush the bread with a little melted butter, and sprinkle with coarse salt.

- 1 package active dry yeast
- 2¼ cups all-purpose flour
- ¼ cup warm water (about 120°)
- 1 cup large-curd low-fat cottage cheese
- 1 tablespoon unsalted butter, melted
- ¼ teaspoon baking soda
- 2 tablespoons sugar
- 1½ teaspoons salt
- ½ teaspoon dill seed
- 2 teaspoons finely minced onion
- ¼ cup packed fresh dill, snipped ¼-inch long
- 1 large egg, lightly beaten, room temperature
  Vegetable-oil cooking spray

1. In the bowl of an electric mixer, gently combine yeast, ¼ cup flour, and water. Let sit until foamy, about 10 minutes. Meanwhile, place the cottage cheese in the top of a double boiler full of boiling water, and stir until warm to the touch, or microwave until warm. Add the melted butter to the yeast mixture, and mix on medium speed for 2 minutes.

2. Add warmed cottage cheese, baking soda, sugar, salt, dill seed, onion, snipped dill, egg, and the remaining dry flour to the yeast mixture, and mix on high speed to make a stiff batter, about 3 minutes. Scrape down the sides of the bowl, cover, and set batter aside in warm place to rise until doubled in bulk, 30 to 40 minutes.

3. Spray an 8-inch cast-iron skillet generously with cooking spray, and set aside. Scrape out the batter, and pour it into the skillet. Spray the plastic wrap with cooking spray, and place over the dough, pressing down on the wrap to even the dough. Lift the plastic wrap so it is not touching surface of dough, and let dough stand in warm place until it doubles, about 25 minutes.

4. Heat the oven to 350°. Remove the plastic wrap, transfer the dough to the oven, and bake until golden brown, about 35 to 40 minutes. If the bread begins to get too dark, cover it loosely with aluminum foil. Remove the pan from the oven, and transfer to a wire rack to cool. Serve the bread warm, cut into wedges.

ABOVE: Golden cottage cheese-dill bread can go from the oven to the table right in its cast-iron skillet.

A dinner plate shows a little bit of everything on the first go-around: a barbecued chicken breast glistening from the spicy peach glaze, a wedge of the dill skillet bread, and spoonfuls of the layered and the macaroni-and-potato salads.

Macaroni-and-Potato Salad

serves 8

Combine two classics to make a delicious summer salad. This dish is best served immediately, while bacon is still warm.

- *3 large all-purpose potatoes (2 pounds), peeled and cut into ¾-inch cubes*
- *½ teaspoon salt, plus more for cooking water*
- *2 cups sugar snap peas (6 ounces)*
- *¼ pound elbow macaroni, cooked al dente and drained*
- *1 pound sliced bacon*
- *½ cup plus 2 tablespoons mayonnaise*
- *3 tablespoons sour cream*
- *1½ tablespoons cider vinegar*
- *¼ teaspoon freshly ground pepper*
- *½ cup loosely packed fresh mint leaves, torn into pieces*

1. Place potatoes in a small stockpot, and cover with cold salted water. Place over high heat; bring to a boil. Reduce heat to medium high, and gently boil potatoes until fork tender, about 7 minutes. Drain in colander; set aside in a large bowl to cool.
2. Fill a small saucepan with salted water, and bring to a boil. Add snap peas, and cook until bright green, about 30 seconds. Drain, and transfer to a bowl of ice water until cool. Drain again, slice in half crosswise diagonally, and add to potatoes along with cooked macaroni.
3. In large skillet, cook bacon until all fat is rendered and the bacon is very crisp. Remove from skillet; set aside on paper towels to drain. When bacon is cool, crumble, and add three-quarters of it to potato mixture; set aside remaining bacon.
4. In medium mixing bowl, whisk together the mayonnaise, sour cream, vinegar, ½ teaspoon salt, and pepper. Pour dressing over the potato mixture, add mint, and toss to combine. Transfer macaroni-and-potato salad to a serving dish; sprinkle top with the remaining bacon. Serve salad immediately, or cover and store in the refrigerator until ready to serve.

Barbecued Chicken Breasts With Spicy Peach Glaze

serves 8

The perfect summer dish, this chicken is even better served cold the next day.

- *1 cup peach preserves or jam*
- *1 large clove garlic, minced (1 teaspoon)*
- *2 tablespoons olive oil*
- *1 tablespoon plus 1 teaspoon soy sauce*
- *1 tablespoon dry mustard*
- *¼ teaspoon cayenne pepper*
- *1 teaspoon salt, plus more to taste*
- *¼ teaspoon freshly ground black pepper, plus more to taste*
- *4 chicken breasts, split (about 5 pounds)*
- *4 ripe peaches, cut in half and pitted*

1. Heat a grill to medium hot. In medium mixing bowl, combine the preserves, garlic, olive oil, soy sauce, dry mustard, cayenne pepper, salt, and black pepper, and mix well to combine.
2. Sprinkle the chicken breasts with additional salt and pepper, and place, skin-side down, on the grill. Cook the chicken about 10 minutes on each side before brushing the upturned side with glaze. Continue cooking the chicken for another 10 to 12 minutes, turning it every 3 to 5 minutes and brushing each upturned side with glaze every time, until chicken is cooked through. Move chicken to oven or a cooler part of grill if it gets too dark before it is cooked through.
3. Place peach halves on grill, cut-side down, and grill for 2 minutes. Turn, and brush tops with glaze. Grill 3 to 4 minutes more, until peaches are soft and cavities fill with juices. Transfer cooked chicken and peaches to a serving platter.

don't forget

- Too many hours of preparation the day of the picnic can spoil the event. Cook as much of the food as possible the day before. Last-minute baking is most comfortably done in the morning hours.

- There can never be too much food at a picnic. Invite your guests to contribute a fruit pie, some of their homemade pickles, or a fresh summer salad. Most people will be happy to bring a favorite dish.

- You can always improvise and add to the meal. The macaroni-and-potato salad lends itself to last-minute additions of whatever vegetable looks fresh, whether asparagus, cucumbers, or beets.

- Involve children in the preparation. Ask them to pick wildflowers, set the table, or fold napkins in a new way: triangles, pleats, or tucked in a glass, so that the corners stick up like a flower.

- Have some insect repellent and citronella candles on hand to ward off any mosquitoes.

- Music. If someone plays the guitar, ask him or her to bring it.

Sweet Corn

serves 8

It is traditional to use milk and sugar to bring out the sweetness in day-old corn. But you can give any corn a boost with this recipe.

2 quarts milk
2 quarts water
1 tablespoon sugar
8 ears corn

In a large stockpot, bring milk, water, and sugar to a boil. Add corn, and cook 3 to 5 minutes, or less.

Cherry Lemonade

serves 6 to 8

Make this drink as sweet—or tart—as you like; just adjust sugar to taste.

1¼ cups freshly squeezed lemon juice (about 12 lemons)
1 cup sugar
3 quarts cold water
1 pound fresh cherries, pitted

In a gallon container, combine lemon juice and sugar until sugar is dissolved. Stir in water and cherries until combined. Serve in glasses filled with ice.

ABOVE: Picking corn is only half of the job; the other half is shucking it and removing all the silk. RIGHT: In a guest's pickup, chairs are last to leave. OPPOSITE: The picnic table—laden with the layered salad, skillet bread, chicken breasts, and cherry lemonade—is covered with a bright yellow cloth and a mix of red and blue napkins—perfect, too, for a Fourth of July celebration.

A June classic: a pie bursting with fresh cherries, topped with a lattice crust. The smaller pie, baked without a crust on top, is peach-raspberry.

Piecrust

makes two 9-inch crusts

This is just the right amount of dough for a 9-inch double-crust pie. You can use the same recipe to make two 4-inch pies or one large open-face pie. Use scraps to make pie tarts. For larger or smaller pies, adjust cooking time accordingly. A fruit filling is usually done when juices bubble. The piecrust should always be golden.

- 2½ cups all-purpose flour
- 1 teaspoon salt
- 1 teaspoon sugar
- ½ pound (2 sticks) cold unsalted butter
- 5 tablespoons ice water

1. Place the flour, salt, and sugar in a food processor, and process for a few seconds to combine. Cut the butter into small pieces, add to flour mixture, and process until mixture resembles coarse meal, about 10 seconds. (To mix the dough by hand, combine flour, salt, and sugar in a large bowl. Using a pastry blender or two knives, cut in butter until mixture resembles coarse meal.)
2. Add ice water in a slow, steady stream, through feed tube of a food processor with machine running, just until the dough holds together. Do not process for more than 30 seconds. (If hand mixing, mix in ice water with a fork until dough comes together.)
3. Divide dough in half, and turn each half out onto a piece of plastic wrap. Press each half into a flattened circle, and wrap in plastic. Refrigerate piecrust for at least 1 hour before using for pies.

Sour-Cherry Pie

makes one 9-inch pie

Sour cherries are usually too tart to eat raw, but they make an excellent pie filling.

- 1 recipe Piecrust (recipe at left)
- 1 large egg
- 1 tablespoon milk
- 7 cups cherries, pitted
- 1 tablespoon freshly squeezed lemon juice
- 1 cup sugar
- 6 tablespoons all-purpose flour
- 2 tablespoons unsalted butter, cut into small pieces

1. On a lightly floured surface, roll out half the dough to ⅛-inch-thick circle, about 13 inches in diameter. Drape dough over a 9-inch pie pan, and transfer to refrigerator to chill for about 30 minutes.
2. Heat oven to 425°. Whisk together the egg and milk, and set aside. Combine the cherries, lemon juice, sugar, and flour, and turn onto chilled bottom crust. Dot with the butter. Roll out the remaining piecrust dough to the same size and thickness. Brush rim of crust with egg wash, place the second piecrust on top, trim to ½ inch over edge of pan, and crimp edges with a fork or your fingers. Transfer to the refrigerator until firm, about 15 minutes. Brush with egg wash, and bake 20 minutes. Reduce heat to 350°, and bake 30 to 40 minutes more. Let cool before serving.

Peach-Raspberry Pie

makes one 9-inch pie

This dessert also tastes good with a crunchy sugary crust: Forgo the egg wash, brush the pastry with cold water, and sprinkle with sugar.

- 1 recipe Piecrust (recipe far left)
- 1 large egg
- 1 tablespoon milk
- 4 pounds peaches (about 8 large), peeled and sliced
- ½ pint raspberries
- ½ cup sugar
- ¼ cup all-purpose flour
- 2 tablespoons unsalted butter, cut into small pieces

1. On a lightly floured work surface, roll out half the dough to ⅛-inch-thick circle, about 13 inches in diameter. Drape dough over a 9-inch pie pan; transfer to refrigerator to chill for about 30 minutes.
2. Heat oven to 425°. Whisk together the egg and milk, and set aside. Combine the peaches, raspberries, sugar, and flour, and turn onto the chilled bottom crust. Dot with the butter. Roll out the remaining piecrust dough to the same size and thickness. Add an extra tablespoon of flour if the peaches are very juicy. Brush the rim of the crust with the egg wash, place the second piecrust on top, trim to ½ inch over edge of pan, and crimp the edges with a fork or your fingers. Transfer pie to the refrigerator until firm, about 15 minutes. Brush with egg wash, and bake for 20 minutes. Reduce heat to 350°, and bake 30 to 40 minutes more. Let cool before serving.

POLYNESIAN
BASH

TROPICAL-FRUIT SALSA AND TARO CHIPS

SEAFOOD SUMMER ROLLS

CRAB-AND-MANGO SUMMER ROLLS

SKEWERED ISLAND SEAFOOD

GREEN-PAPAYA SALAD

HACKED COCONUT CHICKEN

TROPICAL DRINKS

BAKED HAWAII

BANANA DUMPLINGS

PASSION-FRUIT CUSTARD

COCONUT-CREAM SANDWICHES

OPPOSITE, CLOCKWISE FROM TOP LEFT: The focal point of the luau—a simple bamboo hut with muted tropical colors for tablecloths and glowing paper lanterns—awaits the first guests. Both the scent and sight of the party's fresh-flower leis transport each guest from the everyday world to a South Pacific paradise. Orchids and paper parasols are frothy embellishments to tropical drinks: a mango-melon colada, a lime-flavored daiquirita, and a blue cloud. Guests go native.

Combining decorations, drinks, and delicacies, the retro fantasy of a Polynesian party comes to life on a Hawaiian beach.

Orchids and hibiscus, papayas and mangoes—some of the most evocative ingredients that make a luau—can all be picked fresh on Maui, the site for this party. But a tropical feast can take place wherever sultry breezes play in the trees (pines will substitute for palms in a pinch). The point is to capture the romance and excitement of the islands, whether on a nearby beach or right in your own backyard. Authenticity is not necessary; follow your own uninhibited sense of fantasy, based on personal visions of a tropical paradise that may draw on Gauguin's Tahitian paintings, scenes from television's *Gilligan's Island,* or a night out at Trader Vic's. The only constants for a Polynesian party are found in the mood: primitive, glamorous, lush, languorous. The menu for this Polynesian evening includes updated versions of what was once called "Hawaiian fun food," dishes that draw on the Pan–Asian cuisines of China, Japan, Korea, Malaysia, Thailand, and the Philippines. The very essence of countercool, this spirited bash can be scored with tiki–style music from the fifties and sixties: Hawaiian slide guitar riffs, Elvis Presley's songs from *Blue Hawaii,* Annette Funicello's lively "Rock-A-Hula Baby" and "Luau Cha Cha Cha." Watch the sun set with a glass of guava-champagne punch or a melon-mango colada. After all, ambience is everything, and escape the name of the game.

TOP, LEFT TO RIGHT: A large, galvanized-steel bucket draped with two novelty-store hula skirts makes a very cool cooler. Fresh guavas are sliced to garnish the champagne punch. Inexpensive oil-filled tiki torches light the shoreline, or can conjure up a sandy beach in a backyard. ABOVE LEFT: Vintage tiki mugs, including this Easter Island model, are often found at flea markets. OPPOSITE: A pail, wrapped in ti leaves and bound with lengths of raffia, becomes an exotic ice bucket; bamboo-handled flatware adds another tropical detail to the buffet.

Tropical-Fruit Salsa

makes 5½ cups

Serve with fish, chicken, or taro chips.

- *1 pound sweet onions, such as Maui, Vidalia, Texas Sweet, or Oso Sweet*
- *2 teaspoons extra-virgin olive oil*
- *1 ripe mango (about ¼ pound), peeled, seeded, and cut into ¼-inch dice*
- *1 ripe papaya (about 1¼ pounds), peeled, seeded, and cut into ¼-inch dice*
- *¼ pineapple, peeled, cored, and cut into ¼-inch dice (about 1 cup)*
- *3 plum tomatoes, cut into ¼-inch dice*
- *1 jalapeño pepper, seeded and finely chopped*
- *2½ tablespoons freshly squeezed lemon juice*
- *2 tablespoons freshly squeezed lime juice*
- *¼ cup coarsely chopped cilantro leaves*
- *½ teaspoon salt*
- *⅛ teaspoon freshly ground pepper*

1. Heat oven to 400°. Halve the onions crosswise; brush the cut sides with oil. Cook, cut-side down, in a roasting pan, until caramelized, 1 hour 20 minutes. Turn onions over, and let cool. Peel onions, and cut into ¼-inch dice.
2. Combine onions with the remaining ingredients. Toss well; cover until serving.

Taro Chips

serves 12 as part of a buffet

Once a staple food in Hawaii, taro—a tuber similar to the potato—is considered a delicacy today and is used to make poi for ceremonies. Choose roots that are firm and smooth.

- *6 cups peanut or vegetable oil*
- *2 large taro roots or 7 Idaho potatoes (about 3½ pounds), peeled*
- *½ teaspoon salt, or to taste*

1. Heat oil in a large, wide saucepan over medium-high heat until temperature registers 375° on a deep-frying or candy thermometer. Slice taro as thinly as possible using a mandolin or vegetable slicer. Fry the taro slices in a single layer without crowding them, until they are crisp and the edges are golden brown, 45 to 60 seconds per side.
2. Transfer chips with a slotted spoon to a paper-towel-lined baking sheet. Blot chips with paper towels and sprinkle with salt. Repeat with all the taro. Serve with Tropical Fruit Salsa.

ABOVE: Taro chips and a tropical salsa of mango, pineapple, papaya, jalapeño pepper, and tomato pair up to make an exotic hors d'oeuvre.

Seafood Summer Rolls

makes 10 rolls or 40 pieces

The wrappers for these rolls are called Vietnamese or Thai rice paper—flat, dry, translucent disks of rice-noodle dough.

1 teaspoon salt
2 ounces rice vermicelli
1 package 8½-inch rice-paper sheets
10 ounces fresh center-cut skinless tuna (ahi)
2 cups loosely packed mizuna or watercress leaves
1 cup loosely packed mint leaves
2 cups tightly packed basil leaves
1 carrot, peeled and julienned
1 small cucumber, peeled, seeded, julienned
  Citrus Dipping Sauce (recipe follows)

1. Bring a pot of water to a boil. Add salt and rice vermicelli; cook until tender, 2 to 3 minutes. Drain, and rinse in cold water.
2. Put rice-paper sheets in a plastic bag to keep from curling; remove 1 sheet at a time. Stack 2 paper towels, one on top of the other, on a work surface. Spray towels with water, and lay a sheet of rice paper on top. Cover with 2 paper towels, spray again, and repeat until you have 10 layers of rice paper. Let stand until rice paper is pliable, 10 to 15 minutes.
3. Cut tuna into ½-by-2½-inch pieces.
4. Place 1 sheet of rice paper on a work surface. Place 2 pieces of tuna end to end across bottom third of rice paper; around them place 3 mizuna leaves, 4 mint leaves, and 3 basil leaves. Leaving ¼-inch border on each side, top with 6 strands each of carrot and cucumber and ¼ cup of vermicelli. Cover with 3 more mizuna leaves, 4 mint leaves, and 3 basil leaves. Roll rice paper into a cylinder, stopping halfway. Fold left and right edges into the middle, and finish rolling.
5. Place roll on a baking sheet lined with plastic wrap, cover, and refrigerate. Repeat entire process, making 10 rolls. To serve, trim ends, and cut rolls into 4 pieces. Chill until ready to serve; serve Citrus Dipping Sauce on the side.

Crab-and-Mango Summer Rolls

makes 10 rolls or 40 pieces

1 pound king-crab legs or 8 ounces lump crabmeat, picked over
1 large ripe mango (about 14 ounces), pitted and peeled
10 Boston lettuce leaves
3 scallions
1 teaspoon salt
2 ounces rice vermicelli
1 package 8½-inch rice-paper sheets
1 cup tightly packed cilantro leaves
1 cup tightly packed mint leaves
  Citrus Dipping Sauce (recipe follows)

1. Remove the meat from crab legs. Slice 5-inch-long strips, cover, and refrigerate.
2. Cut mango into strips ½ inch by 2½ inches. Cut lettuce leaves in half, lengthwise, and discard the center ribs. Trim each scallion into two 5-inch lengths; slice lengthwise into very thin strips.
3. Place salt and rice vermicelli in a pot of boiling water, and cook until tender, 2 to 3 minutes. Drain; rinse in cold water.
4. Transfer rice paper to a plastic bag; remove 1 sheet at a time. Stack 2 paper towels, one on top of the other, on a work surface. Dampen slightly using a spray bottle of water; lay a sheet of rice paper on top. Cover with 2 more damp paper towels; repeat until you have 10 layers. Let stand until pliable, 10 to 15 minutes.
5. Across bottom third of 1 sheet of rice paper, place 2 pieces of lettuce, 4 cilantro leaves, 4 mint leaves, 1 piece crab (if using lump crabmeat, 2 tablespoons), 2 pieces of mango (end to end), and ¼ cup vermicelli. Cover with 4 strips of scallion, 4 cilantro leaves, and 4 mint leaves. Roll rice paper into a cylinder, stopping halfway. Fold left and right sides into the middle; finish rolling.
6. Place on a baking sheet lined with plastic wrap, cover, and refrigerate. Repeat entire process, making 10 rolls. To serve, trim ends with a sharp knife and cut roll into 4 pieces. Serve Citrus Dipping Sauce on the side.

Citrus Dipping Sauce

makes about 1 cup

⅓ cup freshly squeezed orange juice
⅓ cup freshly squeezed lime juice
¼ cup low-sodium soy sauce
1 tablespoon Chinese dark sesame oil
⅛ teaspoon freshly ground pepper
2 scallions, ends trimmed and thinly sliced

In small bowl, whisk together orange and lime juices, soy sauce, sesame oil, and pepper; add scallions. Serve with the Seafood Summer Rolls and with the Crab-and-Mango Summer Rolls.

ABOVE: Orchids and an array of fruit, including a lug of bananas, make a natural island centerpiece.

Skewered Island Seafood

serves 12 as part of a buffet

Seafood can be threaded onto lemongrass or sugarcane skewers to add flavor and sweetness.

  2 *pounds jumbo shrimp (about 24)*
 2½ *pounds large sea scallops (about 36)*
 2½ *pounds fresh center-cut skinless tuna (ahi)*
100 *ten-inch wooden skewers (fewer if using lemongrass or sugar-cane skewers)*
     Green-Curry Marinade (recipe follows)
 2½ *limes*
  1 *teaspoon salt, or to taste*
  ½ *teaspoon freshly ground pepper*

1. Peel and devein shrimp, leaving tails intact. Remove muscles from scallops. Cut tuna in ¾-by-1-by-1¾-inch pieces.
2. Pour 1½ cups green-curry marinade into a nonreactive dish; cover and refrigerate remaining 1¼ cups of marinade. Place seafood in marinade; turn to coat both sides. Cover, and refrigerate for 1 hour.
3. Heat grill to medium hot. Place wooden skewers in cold water; soak for at least 30 minutes. Skewer each shrimp, tail-end first, and each scallop onto a wooden skewer. (If using sugarcane, cut stalks into thin 10-inch skewers with 1 pointed end, and thread a shrimp on each. If using lemongrass, trim the bases of 18 stalks, remove tough leaves, and halve stalks crosswise. Trim tapered ends to a point, and skewer 1 scallop on each.)
4. Halve the limes; cut each half into 8 wedges. Thread 1 piece of the tuna and 1 lime wedge onto each wooden skewer. Discard marinade.
5. Season seafood with salt and pepper; grill until lightly charred, 2 to 3 minutes per side for shrimp, 4 to 5 per side for scallops, and 1½ to 2 per side for tuna. Serve immediately with the reserved 1¼ cups of marinade as a dipping sauce.

Green-Curry Marinade

makes about 2¾ cups

  3 *stalks lemongrass*
  1 *cup firmly packed cilantro leaves*
  2 *large shallots, peeled*
  2 *medium cloves garlic, peeled*
  3 *scallions, both ends trimmed*
  ⅓ *cup firmly packed basil leaves*
  2 *kaffir-lime leaves, roughly chopped*
  4 *jalapeño peppers, stemmed and seeded*
  1 *teaspoon freshly grated ginger*
  1 *tablespoon ground coriander*
  1 *tablespoon ground cumin*
  3 *tablespoons vegetable oil*
  ¼ *teaspoon salt*
  ¼ *teaspoon freshly ground pepper*
 1¼ *cups canned coconut milk*

1. Discard all but bottom 5 inches of the lemongrass. Peel off the tough outer leaves, trim bases, and slice stalks crosswise into 1-inch pieces; place in a food processor or blender with all remaining ingredients except coconut milk; purée, about 30 seconds.
2. Transfer the purée to a medium skillet over medium-low heat. Cook until the ingredients release their aroma, about 3 minutes. Slowly whisk in coconut milk until well combined. Remove from heat, and set aside to cool.

The pupu platter combines shapes, tastes, and scents of the islands: grilled ahi and shrimp on sugarcane, summer rolls of crab and mango or ahi and vegetables, scallops on lemongrass skewers, and hacked coconut chicken, all served atop broad-leaved ti leaves.

Green-Papaya Salad

serves 12 as part of a buffet

8   ounces string beans, stem ends trimmed

2   teaspoons salt
    Ice water for bath

3   plum tomatoes (about ½ pound)

¼   cup roasted, unsalted peanuts

2   large green (unripe) papayas (about 1
    pound each), peeled and seeded

¼   cup Thai fish sauce

¼   cup freshly squeezed lemon juice

¼   cup freshly squeezed lime juice

2   tablespoons sugar

1   teaspoon minced garlic

2   teaspoons red-pepper flakes

¼   cup roughly chopped cilantro leaves

1. Add beans and salt to a saucepan of boiling water; cook until bright green and just tender, about 2 minutes. Transfer to an ice-water bath. Drain again, and pat beans dry. Cut in half crosswise, then again, lengthwise.

2. Halve the tomatoes lengthwise, and remove the seeds. Slice the halves into ⅛-inch strips. Roughly chop all but 2 tablespoons of peanuts.

3. Julienne papaya, using a mandolin. Toss in a bowl with beans, tomatoes, chopped peanuts, fish sauce, lemon and lime juices, sugar, garlic, red-pepper flakes, and 3 tablespoons cilantro. Garnish with remaining 2 tablespoons peanuts and a tablespoon of cilantro; serve.

Guests will delightedly snatch up individual servings of green-papaya salad; served in the avocado skins, the salad is a charmingly natural addition to a luau and can be easily carried away from the buffet table.

Hacked Coconut Chicken

serves 12 as part of a buffet

½ *cup guava or apricot jam*

1 *tablespoon tamarind concentrate (available in Indian markets)*

¼ *cup Dijon mustard*

½ *cup canned coconut milk*

¼ *cup canned papaya or guava juice, or
freshly squeezed orange juice*

2 *tablespoons curry powder*

¼ *heaping teaspoon cayenne pepper*

2 *whole split chicken breasts, skinned*

1 *cup shredded sweetened coconut*

30 *to 35 ten-inch wooden skewers*

1. Press jam through a strainer. Combine jam with all the ingredients except chicken and coconut in pan over medium-low heat. Cook, stirring occasionally, until marinade reduces to about 1 cup, 15 minutes.

2. Place 1 chicken piece, flesh-side down, on plastic wrap; cover with more wrap. Using a meat mallet or flat side of a heavy cleaver, flatten chicken slightly. Repeat with remaining chicken pieces.

3. Place chicken in a nonreactive dish, and add ⅔ cup marinade; coat both sides. Cover, and refrigerate 2 hours or overnight. Refrigerate remaining ⅓ cup marinade, covered.

4. Heat oven to 350°. Toast coconut on a baking sheet, turning occasionally, until golden brown, 6 to 8 minutes. Set aside.

5. Heat grill to medium hot. Let the chicken stand at room temperature for 30 minutes. Grill until lightly charred, 4 to 5 minutes per side, brushing with marinade several times.

6. Pull bones out of each breast; slice breasts into fifths; halve the larger pieces. Place each piece of chicken on a wooden skewer; brush with reserved ⅓ cup marinade. Sprinkle chicken with toasted coconut.

good thing

Tiki Lighting To lend a tropical ambience to the buffet table and the bar, make a variety of tiki-inspired lights. To make the hurricane lamps (1), tie bamboo sticks together with raffia, stalk by stalk, and wrap around cylindrical glass vases; tie off with raffia. Votive candle-size versions (2) are made with sushi mats and tied with fishing line. To make the tiki lanterns hanging in the buffet hut on page 112, begin with three vertical 20-inch and three horizontal 14-inch bamboo sticks for each of the four sides. Wire each set of six sticks into a windowpane shape. Wire the four windowpane panels together into a cubelike frame. Wire two 20-inch bamboo sticks into an "x," and wire to the four corners of the top of the frame. Conceal the wires (3) by wrapping with raffia. Glue a double thickness of colored tissue paper in place on the inside of the frame (4) for the lantern walls. From the center of "x," hang lantern over a 25- or 40-watt bulb.

Guava-Champagne Punch

serves 12

Guava nectar is sold in cans or as frozen concentrate in Latino groceries and some supermarkets.

2 quarts chilled guava nectar

2 bottles chilled champagne or sparkling wine

3 fresh guavas, cut into ⅛-inch-thick slices for garnish, optional

Combine guava nectar and champagne in a punch bowl. Add guava; serve over ice.

Mango-Melon Colada

makes 2 drinks

⅓ cantaloupe, peeled, seeded, and cut into chunks (about 2 cups)

1 mango, peeled, seeded, and cut into chunks (about 1½ cups)

3 tablespoons cream of coconut

2 tablespoons freshly squeezed lime juice

2 tablespoons superfine sugar

4 ounces light rum

Process all the ingredients and 2 cups crushed ice in blender until thick and smooth, 20 seconds. Divide between two tall glasses, and serve immediately.

Blue Cloud

makes 2 drinks

2 large scoops vanilla- or piña colada-flavored frozen yogurt

1½ ounces blue curaçao

2½ ounces light rum

1 tablespoon freshly squeezed lime juice

2 tablespoons superfine sugar

Process all the ingredients and 2 cups crushed ice in blender until thick and smooth, 20 seconds. Divide between two tall glasses, and serve immediately.

Lime Daiquirita

makes 2 drinks

4 large limes

4 ounces light rum

2 ounces orange-flavored liqueur, such as Triple Sec or Cointreau

3 tablespoons superfine sugar

1. Grate 1 teaspoon zest from 1 lime into a cocktail shaker. Cut the limes in half, and squeeze juice into a measuring cup; you should have about 4 ounces.
2. Add 2 cups ice cubes, lime juice, rum, orange liqueur, and sugar to the shaker; cover, and shake well. Strain into two glasses filled with crushed ice; serve.

Baked Hawaii

serves 12

A tropical take on Baked Alaska, this dessert can be completely assembled up to one day in advance. Instead of using an oven, carefully use a propane torch to brown the meringue, if desired.

25 *thin chocolate cookies (to yield 1¼ cups of crumbs)*

4 *pints sorbet and frozen yogurt in assorted tropical flavors, such as mango, piña colada, lemon, or passion fruit*

1½ *cups sugar*

6 *large egg whites, room temperature*

1½ *teaspoons pure vanilla extract*

2 *tablespoons blue curaçao*

1. Process the cookies into fine crumbs in a food processor, about 45 seconds. Reserve ¼ cup crumbs for garnish. Line a 2½-quart dessert mold with plastic wrap, allowing it to hang over the edges by 6 inches; chill in freezer. Let sorbets and yogurts soften slightly in refrigerator.
2. Place mold in a bowl of ice. Layer ices into mold a half-pint at a time, pressing down with a ladle. Smooth each layer with a rubber spatula, and sprinkle with cookie crumbs. Continue layering until ices are used. Cover; freeze overnight.
3. Remove the mold from freezer. Gather edges of plastic wrap together, and lift the ices out of the mold; invert molded ices onto baking pan, and remove the plastic wrap. Return to freezer.
4. Combine sugar and ½ cup water in a small saucepan, stirring gently with a metal spoon. Cover; cook over medium-high heat until the sugar dissolves, 5 to 6 minutes. Uncover, and place a candy thermometer in syrup. Raise heat to high; boil rapidly until the temperature reaches 248° (firm-ball stage), 1 to 2 minutes.
5. While sugar is heating, beat egg whites in bowl of an electric mixer with whisk attachment at low speed until foamy, about 2 minutes. Gradually increase speed to medium high, and beat until soft peaks begin to form, 2 to 2½ minutes. Reduce speed to low, and add hot syrup in a steady stream. Increase speed to medium high, and continue beating until whites are shiny, stiff, and hold a peak, about 2 minutes. Do not overbeat. Increase speed to high, add vanilla, and beat for 15 seconds more. Transfer to another bowl, and let cool for about 5 minutes, folding gently 1 or 2 times.
6. Remove ices from freezer. Working fast, cover entire surface with meringue. Freeze for at least 1 hour and up to 1 day.
7. When ready to serve the dessert, heat the oven to 500°. Bake the dessert on the lowest rack of the oven until meringue has browned all over, 3 to 4 minutes (don't worry if the ices melt a bit). Transfer dessert to a serving platter; scatter reserved ¼ cup cookie crumbs almost all the way around the base, leaving a small gap; spoon the blue curaçao into the gap, creating a miniature lagoon.

ABOVE: Baked Hawaii, a mountain of tropical-flavored sorbet covered in meringue, rises up from a black-sand beach made of chocolate cookie crumbs; a splash of blue curaçao on the plate suggests a Pacific tidal pool. OPPOSITE: A single hibiscus adorns the guava-champagne punch, a less potent alternative to many other cocktails.

Banana Dumplings

makes 20

1 tablespoon toasted sesame seeds
20 wonton wrappers
1 large ripe banana, sliced into very thin
   rounds
3 tablespoons unsalted butter
2 tablespoons honey

1. Toast sesame seeds in a small skillet over medium heat, shaking pan, until golden brown, about 2 to 3 minutes.

2. Lay 1 wonton wrapper on work surface; place 3 slices of banana off its center. Dip a finger in cold water, and wet edges of wonton wrapper; fold wrapper into a triangle, and press down on the edges to seal. Place on a parchment-lined baking sheet, and cover loosely with plastic wrap. Repeat the process with the remaining wrappers and banana.

3. Melt 1 tablespoon butter in a medium skillet over medium heat, and add as many banana dumplings as will fit comfortably. Cook until golden brown, about 2 minutes on each side. Transfer to a baking pan in a warm oven. Repeat the process until all dumplings are cooked. Transfer to serving platter, sprinkle with sesame seeds, and drizzle with honey. Serve immediately.

Passion-Fruit Custard

makes 15

16 passion fruit
1½ cups heavy cream
4 large egg yolks, lightly beaten
½ cup plus 2 tablespoons sugar
1½ tablespoons cold unsalted butter
   Ice water for bath

1. Using a serrated knife, cut the passion fruit in half lengthwise. Scoop flesh into a sieve set over a small bowl; reserve 15 of the shell halves; discard the rest. Press fruit through strainer; discard solids. Scoop pink membrane from shells. Trim a bit of skin off the shells' rounded side to give them a flat base.

2. Bring cream to a boil over medium-high heat. Remove from heat immediately.

3. Fill small stockpot a quarter full with water; bring to a boil. Reduce heat to low; let simmer. Combine egg yolks and ½ cup sugar in heatproof medium bowl, and place over simmering water. Whisk mixture until pale and thick, 3 to 4 minutes.

4. Whisking constantly, add cream and half passion-fruit juice to the egg-and-sugar mixture. Stir constantly with wooden spoon until mixture thickens and coats the back of the spoon, about 10 minutes.

5. Strain mixture immediately into a bowl. Whisk in the butter, cut into small pieces, until melted; whisk in remaining passion-fruit juice. Place bowl over ice-water bath. Stir occasionally until cool. Place passion-fruit shells on baking pan; fill them with custard. Cover; refrigerate for at least 1 hour.

6. Heat broiler. Sprinkle the remaining 2 tablespoons sugar over the shells. Broil on highest rack until sugar caramelizes, about 30 seconds. Serve immediately.

Coconut-Cream Sandwiches

makes 30 to 35

1¼ cups whole blanched almonds (7 ounces)
1 cup superfine sugar
2 large egg whites
1¼ teaspoon pure almond extract
1½ cups heavy cream
1¼ cups shredded sweetened coconut

1. Heat oven to 350°. Process almonds and 2 tablespoons sugar in food processor to a fine powder, about 1 minute. Transfer to bowl of electric mixer with paddle attachment, and add remaining sugar, egg whites, and 1 teaspoon almond extract; combine on medium-low speed.

2. Drop rounded teaspoonfuls of dough on a parchment-lined baking sheet, 1 to 2 inches apart. Bake until very light brown, 15 to 17 minutes. Place sheet on a wire rack. Let cookies cool on sheet for 15 minutes before transferring to racks to cool completely.

3. Meanwhile, pour cream and remaining ¼ teaspoon almond extract into a chilled metal bowl; whip cream until soft peaks form. Place a heaping teaspoon of the whipped cream on the underside of each cookie, and sprinkle with coconut. Serve immediately, or refrigerate for up to 2 hours until ready to serve.

Sweet endings to a voluptuous
feast include passion-fruit custard,
coconut-cream sandwich cookies,
and banana dumplings with honey.

BIRTHDAY PARTY

SALMON BIRTHDAY SNAPPERS

SAUSAGE PROFITEROLES

SMOKED-TROUT BRANDADE

GRILLED TENDERLOIN AU POIVRE

PARSLEY POTATO CHIPS

TOMATO PIE

ROSÉ-WINE PUNCH

BUTTERCRUNCH CHOCOLATE-

TRUFFLE LAYER CAKE

OPPOSITE: The pink-and-green color scheme is carried throughout the decorations, presents, and party favors; tubes of bubble-blowing soap are tissue-wrapped like party snappers, and old-fashioned candies are bundled in cellophane.

A celebration of two birthdays—a grandmother's and grandson's—is a doubly festive occasion for a close-knit family.

One-year-old Charlie Symonds and his grandmother Madge Miller are sharing a single birthday party, and all the pleasures of the day will be multiplied—two cakes, more guests, twice the presents. Madge has invited family and friends to the Millers' home on Long Island, New York. Husband Martin, daughters Darcy and Jennifer, and son-in-law Geoffrey are the cohosts. Darcy, who is the weddings editor of *Martha Stewart Living*, has designed the party with a hot-pink and icy-green color scheme. The children have the wide lawn to sit on, the adults a proper table and chairs beneath a grand weeping willow. A separate dessert table has been covered with a tent of gossamer mosquito netting to protect the sweets from inquisitive insects. The joy of this particular party lies in the intermingling of generations: Adults take their turns on the swing; children clamber onto their parents' laps, nibbling on homemade potato chips; and everyone has the chance to blow bubbles. The menu—witty reinventions of classic cookout fare—spans the generations' appetites, for it is food that the children can recognize and the adults can savor. The little sausage profiteroles bring back memories of pigs-in-blankets. Slices of rare tenderloin au poivre, sophisticated stand-ins for hamburgers, are eaten on mini homemade buns. Presents are opened when the spirit moves, but clearly the greatest gift is the party itself.

TOP, LEFT TO RIGHT: Crumbs disappear into the grass—birds will happily take over clean-up duties—while soap bubbles scatter to the wind. Corn cobs, easier to handle when put on sticks of licorice root, await a turn on the grill. Darcy's hand-drawn cards for Madge and Charlie. ABOVE LEFT: Martin, Madge, Charlie, Jennifer, Geoffrey, and Darcy. OPPOSITE: Roses, zinnias, and ranunculuses— in hues of scarlet, orange, and magenta—offer a shock of color on a long table surrounded by green painted chairs and set with jadeite and white dishes.

Easily grasped by hands both big and small, the finger food includes smoked-trout brandade, sausage profiteroles, and salmon snappers.

Salmon Birthday Snappers

serves 8 to 10

Choose smoked salmon that is not too salty; have it sliced evenly and thinly.

½ cup whipped cream cheese
½ ounce sun-dried yellow or red tomato halves (about 7 halves), cut into ⅛-inch dice
1 tablespoon finely snipped fresh dill
  Salt and freshly ground pepper to taste
½ European cucumber (a long, skinny variety available in supermarkets), peeled and seeded
8 ounces smoked salmon, thinly sliced
¼ bunch frisée (1 cup picked)

1. In a medium bowl, combine the cream cheese, tomatoes, and dill. Season with salt and pepper. Transfer cream-cheese mixture to a pastry bag fitted with a plain #12 Ateco round tip; set aside.
2. Cut the cucumber into ¼-by-1¼-inch julienne, and set aside. Cut the salmon into 1¼-by-2¼-inch rectangles, and place on a clean work surface. Pipe a line of the cream-cheese filling across bottom edge of salmon, place a cucumber baton on top, and roll up from bottom. Insert a small piece of the frisée at each end, and transfer to a tray lined with parchment paper. Repeat piping-and-rolling process until all the salmon slices and filling are used. Wrap with plastic wrap, and store in the refrigerator until ready to serve.

Sausage Profiteroles

serves 8 to 10

1 red bell pepper, roasted, peeled, and seeded
1½ tablespoons olive oil
½ cup finely chopped onions
1 clove garlic, minced
8 ounces chicken, turkey, veal, or pork sausage, casing removed
1 recipe Cream-Puff Pastry (recipe follows)
¼ cup flat-leaf parsley

1. Heat oven to 350°. Cut pepper into half-inch squares; set aside. Heat olive oil in a medium skillet over medium-high heat. Add onions and garlic; cook until translucent, about 7 minutes. Add the sausage, breaking into small pieces with spoon. Cook until sausage is cooked through, about 8 minutes (longer for pork).
2. Slice cream puffs crosswise. Spoon about 1 teaspoon of sausage filling into the bottom half, add a piece of red pepper, then replace the top half. Transfer the profiteroles to a baking sheet, place in the oven, and bake until warm, about 2 minutes. Garnish each with a parsley leaf, and serve immediately.

Cream-Puff Pastry

makes about 30

Cream puffs can be made in advance, and frozen in resealable bags. When ready to use, defrost and warm in a 350° oven for about three minutes, until crisp.

4 tablespoons unsalted butter, cut into small pieces
  Pinch of salt
½ cup all-purpose flour
3 large eggs
1 large egg white

1. Heat oven to 375°. Line a baking sheet with parchment paper, and set aside. Combine butter, salt, and ½ cup water in a small saucepan, and place over medium heat. Cook until the butter is melted and water just comes to a boil.
2. Remove from heat, add flour, and stir rapidly. Return to heat, and cook, stirring constantly, until mixture comes together and pulls away from sides of saucepan, about 5 minutes. Remove saucepan from heat, and let cool for 5 minutes.
3. Add the eggs one at a time, beating until they are completely incorporated and the pastry is smooth. Transfer pastry to a bag fitted with a small coupler. Pipe about ½ tablespoon of the pastry into a mound on the prepared baking sheet;

continue piping until all pastry is used, spacing mounds about 1½ inches apart. Combine the egg white with 1 tablespoon of water, and brush the top of each mound with egg wash. Bake until the puffs are golden brown all over, about 30 minutes. Remove from the oven, and transfer to wire rack; let cool completely.

Smoked-Trout Brandade

serves 8 to 10

Smoked whitefish can be substituted for the trout in this recipe.

8 ounce smoked boneless trout, skin removed
1 tablespoon finely chopped shallots
9 tablespoons heavy cream
2 teaspoons bottled white horseradish
  Pinch freshly ground pepper
1 ficelle or baguette, cut into ⅓-inch-thick slices, toasted
30 fresh-picked small chervil leaves, for garnish

Place all the ingredients, except toast and chervil, in a food processor, and purée. Spread about ½ tablespoon trout purée onto each slice of the toast. Garnish each slice with a small sprig of chervil, and serve immediately.

Grilled Tenderloin au Poivre

serves 8 to 10

Ask your butcher to trim the silver skin, the side piece, and all the fat off the filet. Don't have the filet tied. Be sure to have one pound of the side piece reserved for the sauce, and the remaining trimmings ground to use for hamburgers.

6½ *pounds beef tenderloin, fully trimmed*
⅓ *cup whole black peppercorns*
2 *tablespoons olive oil*
⅓ *cup finely chopped shallots (2 small)*
1 *teaspoon finely chopped garlic (1 large clove)*
1 *cup dry red wine*
⅓ *cup brandy*
6 *tablespoons demi-glace or unsalted beef stock*
¼ *cup heavy cream*
   Salt and freshly ground pepper to taste
1 *tablespoon finely chopped flat-leaf parsley*
½ *tablespoon finely chopped fresh rosemary*
½ *tablespoon finely chopped fresh thyme*
½ *pound assorted baby greens, including radicchio and endive (15 cups)*
1 *bunch chives, for garnish*

1. Heat grill to high. Let tenderloin stand at room temperature for 30 minutes. Place peppercorns in a resealable freezer bag. Using a meat pounder or a mallet, crush the peppercorns until coarse.
2. Pour the olive oil into a large skillet, and place over high heat. Cut reserved pound of filet trimmings into one-inch pieces. Add the trimmings to the hot oil, and cook, turning frequently, until the meat is browned and cooked through, about 6 minutes. Remove and discard the trimmings. Pour off all but 1 tablespoon of the oil. Reduce heat to low.
3. Add the shallots and garlic; cook until translucent and soft, about 10 minutes. Add wine and brandy, raise the heat to high, and cook, stirring up any brown bits with a wooden spoon. Cook until wine is reduced by two-thirds. Add demi-glace and cream, season with salt and pepper,

and cook until slightly thickened, about 6 minutes. Reduce heat to medium high, stir in parsley, rosemary, and thyme, and cook for 1 minute. Turn off the heat.
4. Sprinkle the tenderloin with salt. Using heels of your palms, press cracked peppercorns into beef; place meat on hot grill.
5. Grill tenderloin until rare, turning while grilling, about 40 to 50 minutes. Remove meat from grill. Transfer to cutting board that has a well; let rest 10 to 15 minutes.
6. Warm sauce over medium heat, and transfer to a gravy boat. Slice the filet; serve immediately, surrounded by the mixed greens. Garnish with chives.

Parsley Potato Chips

serves 8 to 10

When making these chips, it is essential to use two perfectly flat baking pans so the potatoes cook evenly.

1 *cup (2 sticks) unsalted butter, melted*
   Salt and freshly ground pepper to taste
6 *large Idaho potatoes (about 2 pounds) peeled*
1 *cup flat-leaf parsley, packed tightly*

1. Heat oven to 400°. Line a baking sheet with parchment paper. Using pastry brush, paint thin, even coating of butter on parchment; sprinkle lightly with salt and pepper.
2. Using a French or Japanese mandolin, slice potatoes lengthwise into even, translucent slices. Place slices ¼ inch apart on buttered parchment. Brush potato slices with butter; leave no streaks or puddles. Place 1 or 2 parsley leaves on top; flatten leaves with fingers. Place a matching-size potato slice on top, flatten with fingers, brush with butter, and lightly sprinkle with salt and pepper. Cover potatoes with piece of parchment paper; place another sheet pan on top. Weight top pan with three bricks or fill pan with raw beans.
3. Bake, rotating the baking pans until potatoes are crisp and golden brown all over, about 6 minutes (check after 3 minutes). Remove from oven, and serve.

TOP: Slices of rare tenderloin au poivre cascade down a bed of fresh greens. ABOVE: Some younger guests go for a wagon ride to see the sights. OPPOSITE: Each potato chip has a parsley sprig baked within, reminiscent of amber.

- Children treasure party favors, lollipops, balloons, birthday cake, and ice cream, but if children lose their party favors, see their balloons burst, or drop their cake on the lawn, they are sometimes inconsolable. A surplus of these items can ameliorate such moments for everyone. A child will see that what seems irreplaceable can, in fact, be replaced.

- Write the children's names on their party favors, so each one feels special and acknowledged.

- Once the birthday cake is cut, serve children first, who are more in need of instant gratification.

- The natural ending of a birthday party is signaled when the younger children grow tired or cranky.

Tomato Pie

serves 8 to 10

To save time, make the dough a day in advance, fit it into the baking pan, and store it, covered, in the refrigerator.

> 1   recipe Pâte Brisée (recipe follows)
> 6   to 7 medium-large ripe tomatoes, sliced ¼ inch thick
> 4   tablespoons olive oil
>   Salt and pepper to taste
> 6   scallions, trimmed, white and light-green parts only
> 1   cup flat-leaf parsley, coarsely chopped
> 3   tablespoons coarsely chopped fresh marjoram
> 2   large cloves garlic, minced

1. Heat oven to 425°. Lightly flour a clean work surface, and roll the pâte brisée into a rectangle 1 inch larger than an 11½-by-17-inch rectangular baking pan. Fit dough into the pan and up the sides; trim edges flush. Place in the refrigerator to chill.
2. Remove pastry from the refrigerator, and pierce the entire surface with a fork. Cover the bottom of the dough with the tomatoes, arranged so they are touching but not overlapping. Drizzle the tomatoes with 2 tablespoons olive oil, and sprinkle with salt and pepper. Bake for 15 minutes. Reduce the oven temperature to 350°, and bake for 10 minutes.
3. Meanwhile, cut scallions into ¼-inch dice, and combine in a small bowl with the parsley, marjoram, and garlic. Scatter the scallion mixture around, but not on top of, the tomatoes. Sprinkle with salt and pepper, and drizzle the scallion mixture with the remaining 2 tablespoons olive oil. Bake until the crust is golden brown, about 20 minutes. Rotate baking pan one time during baking. Remove from oven; transfer to wire rack to cool. Serve with Grilled Tenderloin au Poivre.

Pâte Brisée

makes 1 tomato-pie crust

> 2½   cups all-purpose-flour
> 1   teaspoon salt
> 1   teaspoon sugar
> 1   cup (2 sticks) cold unsalted butter, cut into small pieces
> ¼   cup ice water

1. Combine flour, salt, and sugar in food processor. Add butter; process until mixture resembles coarse meal, 10 seconds.
2. Add ice water in a slow, steady stream through feed tube of a food processor with machine running until the dough holds together, no more than 30 seconds.
3. Turn dough onto piece of plastic wrap. Press into a flattened rectangle, wrap in plastic, and refrigerate at least 1 hour.

Mini Hamburger Buns

makes 15

The dough can be divided in half and frozen. When ready to use, thaw dough at room temperature, about four hours, or overnight in refrigerator, then resume recipe at step four.

> ½   cup warm milk (about 110°)
> ½   cup warm water (about 110°)
> 1½   tablespoons sugar
> 1   tablespoon active dry yeast
> 3   large egg yolks
> 1½   teaspoons salt
> 3   tablespoons unsalted butter, melted and cooled
> 2¾   cups bread flour
>   Vegetable oil for bowl
> 1   large egg white

1. In bowl of an electric mixer, combine milk, water, and sugar. Sprinkle yeast on top. Let stand until mixture is foamy, about 10 minutes. Using paddle attachment, add egg yolks, salt, butter, and flour; mix on low speed for 2 minutes. Change to dough hook; beat until dough

is smooth, soft, and does not stick to fingers when squeezed, about 5 minutes.

2. Transfer dough from mixer to clean surface. Knead into ball, and place in a bowl brushed with olive oil. Cover securely with plastic; let stand in a warm place until dough is doubled, about 45 minutes. Heat oven to 400°. Line a baking sheet with parchment.

3. Punch back the dough, and divide into fifteen 1¼-ounce balls, 1½ inches in diameter. Loosely cover dough balls with plastic wrap. Using both hands, roll dough back and forth to form a 1-inch-thick-by-12-inch-long coil. Tie dough into a loose knot; place on prepared baking pan. Loosely cover with plastic wrap. Repeat shaping process until all the dough is used up. Let stand in a warm spot to rise for 10 minutes.

4. In a small bowl, combine egg white and 1 tablespoon water. Brush tops of rolls with mixture. Bake the rolls until deep golden brown, rotating pan one time while baking, about 15 minutes. Remove from oven, and transfer to wire rack to cool.

Rosé-Wine Punch

serves 8 to 10

For a fruitier punch, let the fruit sit in the wine overnight. When ready to serve, strain wine, and add freshly sliced fruit.

- ¼ *cantaloupe, peeled*
- 1 *small peach, pitted*
- 1 *small nectarine, pitted*
- 2 *bottles chilled, dry rosé wine*
- 6 *tablespoons sugar*
- 1½ *cups golden or red raspberries*

Slice cantaloupe, peach, and nectarine into bite-size pieces. Pour wine into a large pitcher, and stir in sugar. Add sliced fruit and raspberries, and refrigerate, covered, for 2 hours.

CLOCKWISE FROM TOP LEFT: Mini hamburgers allow young guests to eat quickly, play, and run back to the table to grab another little bite. A fresh tomato pie, dotted with scallions and herbs, is a summertime improvisation of a pizza. The rosé-wine punch gets its fruity flavor from peaches, nectarines, and raspberries. On the deck, mothers have a moment to visit while children play on the lawn.

Buttercrunch Chocolate-Truffle Layer Cake

serves 10

The quantities in these recipes can be cut in half for the smaller cake; baking time should be reduced by five to ten minutes or until a cake tester inserted into center comes out clean. Serve with ice cream.

- *2 cups (4 sticks) unsalted butter, room temperature, plus more for pans*
- *4 cups all-purpose flour, plus more for pans*
- *1 tablespoon baking powder*
- *¼ teaspoon baking soda*
- *½ teaspoon salt*
- *2 cups superfine sugar*
- *6 large eggs, room temperature*
- *1 teaspoon pure vanilla extract*
- *1¼ cups milk*
- *1 recipe Chocolate-Truffle Filling (recipe follows)*
- *4½ cups cracked Buttercrunch (12 ounces; recipe follows)*

1. Heat the oven to 350°. Butter three 9-inch cake pans; line bottoms with parchment. Butter parchment. Dust inside of cake pan with flour, tapping out excess, and set aside. Sift together flour, baking powder, baking soda, and salt; set aside.
2. In bowl of electric mixer, using paddle attachment, combine butter and sugar, and beat on medium-high speed until light and fluffy. Add eggs one at a time, beating to incorporate each egg. Beat in vanilla. Add the flour mixture and milk, alternating between the two, beginning and ending with flour mixture, until combined.
3. Divide batter evenly among the three prepared cake pans. Bake, rotating pans until each cake is golden and cake tester inserted into center of cake comes out clean, about 30 minutes. Let cakes cool on a wire rack for 5 minutes. Remove cakes from the pans, and return to rack to cool, tops up.
4. To assemble, remove papers from bottoms of cakes. Using a serrated knife, trim the top of each cake to a level sur-face. Place one cake layer on a cardboard cake round; spread with 1¼ cups cake filling, and repeat with second layer of cake; top with third layer. Cover sides of cake with remaining buttercrunch choco-late-truffle filling. Spread remaining 1¼ cups plain chocolate filling on top layer.
5. Place a handful of cracked butter-crunch in the palm of your hand, and gently press the candy into sides of cake until completely coated. Fill in any blank spots with remaining buttercrunch pieces. Decorate top as desired, and serve.

Chocolate-Truffle Filling

makes enough filling for one 9-inch layer cake

- *2 cups heavy cream*
- *24 ounces best-quality bittersweet chocolate*
- *4 tablespoons unsalted butter, room temperature*
- *2 teaspoons pure vanilla extract*
- *2 cups finely chopped Buttercrunch (6 ounces; recipe follows)*

1. Heat cream over medium-high heat until just before it boils, 5 to 6 minutes. Meanwhile, chop chocolate into 2-inch pieces, transfer to a food processor, and pulse until chocolate is finely chopped.
2. With the food processor running, pour in hot cream, processing until chocolate is melted, about 1 minute. Turn off; add butter and vanilla, pulsing until combined. Transfer mixture to a large metal bowl, and let stand in a very cool place, stirring occasionally, until cold and slightly stiff, about 1 hour. Using a whisk, whip filling until lightened, 2 to 3 minutes.
3. Remove 1¼ cups of filling, and set aside. This will be used to frost top layer of cake. To the remaining filling, stir in chopped buttercrunch (one-third of the recipe) until combined. This will be used for the filling between the layers and the sides of the cake.

Buttercrunch

fills and decorates one 9-inch layer cake

Just before buttercrunch reaches desired temperature, place prepared baking pan over medium-low heat to warm. This pre-vents buttercrunch from cooling too quick-ly when transferring to pan and allows candy to flow more evenly and smoothly.

- *1½ cups sugar*
- *1½ cups (3 sticks) unsalted butter*
- *Vegetable oil for pan*

1. Lightly oil one 16-by-12-inch baking pan; set aside. In a heavy medium saucepan, combine sugar, butter, and 4½ table-spoons water; place over medium-high heat. Insert a candy thermometer. Cook mixture, stirring constantly, until the tem-perature reaches hard-crack stage, 300°, about 17 minutes.
2. Remove from heat, and immediately pour onto prepared baking pan, rotating the pan to spread buttercrunch evenly. Transfer the pan to a wire rack; let stand until completely cool and hard.
3. Gently tap the pan against a corner of a hard surface to crack candy. Remove candy from pan, and divide into thirds. Working on first two-thirds of butter-crunch (12 ounces), place one piece at a time in the palm of your hand, and hit buttercrunch with back of a heavy soup spoon to crack into one-quarter- to one-half-inch pieces. These will be used to decorate the cake. Set aside. Using a sharp knife, chop the remaining third (6 ounces) of the buttercrunch into one-eighth-inch pieces for filling. Set aside.

Each birthday cake has three buttery layers, thick chocolate frosting, and a spiky butercrunch "crust"; instead of candles, which usually don't stay lighted outdoors, miniature flags made from wired ribbon and glued to bamboo skewers bedeck the festive cakes.

THE GUIDE

Items pictured but not listed are from private collections. Addresses and telephone numbers of sources may change prior to or following publication, as may price and availability of any item.

LOUISIANA OUTDOOR LUNCH

Special thanks to the Parlange family, Virginia Lambert, and Alton Joseph. Thanks also to Sara Gummow and to Margo Bouanchaud of Unique Cuisine Catering, 5358 Government Street, Baton Rouge, LA 70806; 504-927-4260.

page 10
Nineteenth-century French hand-blown-glass **fly catcher** from Lucullus, 610 Chartres Street, New Orleans, LA 70130; 504-528-9620.

pages 12 to 21
Embroidered Irish linen **tablecloth/bed-spread,** $460, from Trouvaille Française, 552 East 87th Street, New York, NY 10128; 212-737-6015. By appointment only. Crystal **champagne flutes** from Lucullus, see above. Calling-card cotton-sateen **chair covers,** made to order, from

Angèle Parlange, 5419 Magazine Street, New Orleans, LA 70115; 504-897-6511. 25½"-square damask **napkins,** $45 each, from Vito Giallo Antiques, 222 East 83rd Street, New York, NY 10028; 212-535-9885. By appointment only.

page 13
Damask cloth with acanthus-leaf swag, $450, from Vito Giallo Antiques, see above.

page 19
Pecan halves, $21 for three pounds, $35 for five pounds (includes shipping and handling), from H.J. Bergeron Pecan Shelling Plant, 10003 False River Road, New Roads, LA 70760; 504-638-7667.

MEDITERRANEAN BUFFET

Special thanks to Carl Doumani and Pam Hunter. Special thanks also to Brenda Bosetti and Jeff Starr of Starr Caterers, 1311 Schramsberg Road, Calistoga, CA 94515; 707-942-9246.

pages 22 to 33
Porcelain **salad plates** by Apilco, $9

each; **cocktail napkins,** $2 each; **dinner napkins,** $3.50 each; **oyster basket,** $53; all from Williams-Sonoma; 800-541-2233 for store locations.

page 24
Nineteenth-century French terra-cotta **confit jars,** $450 to $1,000, from St. Helena Antiques, 1231 Main Street, St. Helena, CA 94574; 707-963-5878.

BIG TEXAS BARBECUE

Special thanks to Marianne Stockebrand and the Chinati Foundation, 1 Cavalry Row, Marfa, TX 79843; 915-729-4362. Special thanks also to Al Micallef, owner, CF Ranch; and Grady Spears, co-owner, Reata Restaurant, Alpine, TX; 915-837-9232.

pages 34 to 45
Donald Judd furniture available through the Donald Judd Estate, 104 South Highland Avenue, Marfa, TX 79843; 213-225-5681. Westerberg **flatware,** $39.95 for a 3-piece setting, from IKEA; 410-931-8940 for East Coast locations, 818-912-1119 for West Coast. Glazed Italian **terra-cotta**

bowls, $250 each, *from Gardens, 1818 West 35th Street, Austin, TX 78703; 512-451-5490.* Glass **votives**, $10, and **iced-tea containers** *from El Plato, 1736 18th Street, San Francisco, CA 94107; 415-621-4487. To the trade only.* Clamp preserve **jars**, $3 to $9, and **Bola pitchers**, $18, *from Cost Plus, 2552 Taylor Street, San Francisco, CA 94133; 415-928-6200.* Awning-striped **napkins** *from Maison et Café, 148 South LaBrea, Los Angeles, CA 90036; 213-935-3157.* Oversize **steak knives** *from Economy Restaurant Fixtures, 1200 Seventh Street, San Francisco, CA 94107; 415-626-5611.* 11¼" **dinner plates** *from Buffalo China, 658 Bailey Avenue, Buffalo, NY 14206; 716-824-8515. To the trade only.*

pages 39 and 43
Dried corn husks, $3.25 per 4 ounces, and **masa harina**, $1.75 per pound, *from Kitchen Market, 218 Eighth Avenue, New York, NY 10011; 212-243-4433.*

VIETNAMESE-THAI FEAST

Special thanks to Mai Pham, author of The Best of Vietnamese and Thai Cooking (Prima Publishing; $18.95).

page 46
Raw silk (MS-3, MS-4), $12 per yard, *from Silk India, 1359 Broadway, Suite 1202, New York, NY 10018; 212-629-0101.* **Silver-plated chargers**, $295 each, *from William Lipton, Ltd., 27 East 61st Street, New York, NY 10021; 212-751-8131.* **Folding stools**, $16.95 each, *from Weiss & Mahoney, 142 Fifth Avenue, New York, NY 10011; 212-675-1915.*

pages 48 and 49
Beer glass, $8.50, *from Coconut Company, 131 Greene Street, New York, NY 10012; 212-539-1940.* Oval **ceramic platter** by Brett, $88; **bamboo sticks**, $10 for a pack of 50; *all from Filamento, 2185 Fillmore Street, San Francisco, CA 94115; 415-931-2224.* Lord Kitchener **folding table** with woven-cane top, $1,270, *from British Khaki, 62 Greene Street, New York, NY 10012; 212-343-2299.* Cesare Rossit glass **compote**, $125, and circa-1930 **decanter** by Carlo Scarpa, $1,600, *from DeVera, 384 Hayes Street, San Francisco, CA 94102; 415-861-8480.* Ceramic soup **bowls** *from Takashimaya, 693 Fifth Avenue, New York, NY 10022;*

212-350-0100. Rattan **butler's tray**, $445, *from Coconut Company, see above.* Green **bamboo candles**, $39.50 to $165, *from William Lipton, Ltd., see above.* Apple-green 3" **square candles**, $18 each, and 4" **round candles**, $25 each, *from Susan Schadt Designs; 800-459-4595.*

page 51
Small **glass bowl**, $30, *from Calvin Klein, 800-294-7978 for store locations.* Green **linen napkin**, $22, *from Henri Bendel, 712 Fifth Avenue, New York, NY 10019; 212-247-1100.* Green **salad plate**, $35, *from Takashimaya, see above.* Green **bamboo chopsticks**, $10 per pair, *from Filamento, see above.* **Wax orange blossoms** *from Bell'occhio, 8 Brady Street, San Francisco, CA 94103; 415-864-4048. No catalog.*

page 52
Green **square plate** *from Dean & DeLuca, 560 Broadway, New York, NY 10012; 800-221-7714 or 212-431-1691.* Small **porcelain bowl**, $24, *from Sara, 952 Lexington Avenue, New York, NY 10021; 212-772-3243.*

page 53
Large **glass bowl**, $75, *from Calvin Klein, see above.*

page 55
Cream **square plate**, $95, *from Felissimo, 10 West 56th Street, New York, NY 10019; 212-247-5656.*

page 58
Ceramic bowls, $100 for set of 5, and small **oval teaspoons**, $15 each, *from Felissimo, see above.*

page 59
Smoked-cedar tray, $33, and **silver-leafed bowl** *from Elements, 102 East Oak Street, Chicago, IL 60611; 312-642-6574.*

SEASIDE DINNER

Special thanks to everyone on Useppa Island, especially Kathe Tanous and Bob Levenson, Thomas and Elizabeth Munz, Carolyn and Rusty Hager, and to the Useppa Island Club, Box 640, Bokeelia, FL 33922; 813-283-1061. Special thanks also to Lisa Hammerquist.

pages 60 to 67
Café chairs, $119 for 2, *from Gardener's*

Eden; 800-822-9600. Roseline Vert **fabric** (33260/5) for tablecloth, $93 per yard, *from Clarence House, 211 East 58th Street, New York, NY 10022; 212-752-2890. To the trade only.* White **dinner plate** *from Wedgwood; 800-677-7860 for nearest retailer.* Silver-plate **flatware** *from Fritz's American Wonder at the Tomato Factory, 2 Somerset Street, Hopewell, NJ 08525; 609-466-9833.* Round **wineglasses**, $49 each, *from Simon Pearce, 500 Park Avenue, New York, NY 10022; 212-421-8801.* **Kerosene lantern**, $65, *from Tent & Trails, 21 Park Place, New York, NY 10007; 212-227-1760.*

page 62
Regatta **beach towels**, $25 each, *from Ralph Lauren Home Collection; 212-642-8700 for store locations.* **Thermos** *from Ruby Beets Antiques, P.O. Box 596, Wainscott, NY 11975; 516-537-2802.*

page 65
Spatter **platter** *from Dean & DeLuca; 800-221-7714.*

SKATING PARTY

Special thanks to the Baughman family.

page 68
Key tags, 25 cents each, *from B&N Hardware, 12 West 19th Street, New York, NY 10011; 212-242-1136.*

page 71
"Muck" **aluminum boxes**, $9 and $18, *from IKEA; 410-931-8940 for East Coast locations, 818-912-1119 for West Coast.*

page 73
12-quart **galvanized-steel buckets**, $5.50 each, *from Ace Hardware; 630-990-6600 for store locations.*

GARDEN HARVEST PARTY

Special thanks to Ina Garten and the Barefoot Contessa, 46 Newtown Lane, East Hampton, NY 11937; 516-324-0240; and garden designer Edwina von Gal.

pages 76 to 87
3" **terra-cotta pots**, 38 cents each, *from Archetique Enterprises, Inc., 123 West*

28th Street, New York, NY 10001; 212-563-8003. **Purple-carrot seeds** *from Garden City Seeds, 778 Highway 93 North, Room 13, Hamilton, MT 59840; 406-961-4837. Free catalog.* **Pattypan squash seeds** *from the Cook's Garden, P.O. Box 535, Londonderry, VT 05148; 800-457-9703 or 802-824-3400. Free catalog.* **Fingerling seed potatoes** *from Ronnigers Seed and Potato Farm, Star Route 51, Moyie Springs, ID 83845; 360-893-8782. Free catalog.*

page 76
Green **wooden bench**, $275, and gray **tables**, $575 for two, *from Hunters & Collectors, Poxabogue Lane, Bridge-hampton, NY 11932; 516-537-4233.*

page 80
Scalloped-edge platter, $85, *from Wolfman-Gold & Good, 117 Mercer Street, New York, NY 10012; 212-431-1888.*

page 87
French pressed-glass **jelly jar**, $35, *from Ad Hoc Softwares, 410 West Broadway, New York, NY 10012; 212-925-2652.*

SOUL-FOOD BRUNCH

Special thanks to Sheila Bridges of Sheila Bridges Designs, Inc., 1925 Seventh Avenue, New York, NY 10026; 212-678-6872. Special thanks also to Elizabeth Wayman.

pages 88 to 99
Antique Lenox **dinner plates**, $900 for set of 12; **Paris porcelain**, $4,500 for 79-piece set; Paris-porcelain **compote**, $295; *all from John Rosselli International, 523 East 73rd Street, New York, NY 10021; 212-772-2137.*

page 90
Amber glass **elliptical bowl**, $175, *from Charterhouse Antiques, 115 Greenwich Avenue, New York, NY 10014; 212-243-4726.*

page 91
Linen panels for tablecloths, $15 to $25 per yard, *from B&J Fabrics, 263 West 40th Street, New York, NY 10018; 212-354-8150.* Vintage-frame rectangular **mirror**, $500, *from Rooms & Gardens, 290 Lafayette Street, New York, NY 10012; 212-431-1297.*

page 95
Chartreuse **tole basket**, $750, *from*

L. Becker Flowers, 217 East 83rd Street, New York, NY 10028; 212-439-6001.

FAMILY COUNTRY PICNIC

pages 100 to 111
Antique **chairs**, $45 to $90, *from The Olde White Church, 220 Oak Street, Hills, IA 52235; 319-679-2337.* French linen **fabric** for tablecloth, $26.95 per yard, and linen **napkins**, $4.95 each, *from Maison et Café, 1148 South La Brea Avenue, Los Angeles, CA 90036; 213-935-3157.* English **ironstone plate**, $25, *from Le Marché de Sion, 700 Seventh Street, San Francisco, CA 94107; 415-255-8845.* Glass **carafe, tumbler, bowl,** and **salt and pepper shakers** *all from Crate & Barrel, 650 Madison Avenue, New York, NY 10022; 800-323-5461 or 212-308-0011.* **Enamelware** *from Fredericksen Hardware, 3029 Fillmore Street, San Francisco, CA 94123; 415-292-2950.*

page 102
Large **glass jar** *from Antique Mall of Iowa City, 507 South Gilbert Street, Iowa City, IA 52245; 319-354-1822.* **Toolbox** *from Kmart; 800-335-6278 for store locations.* **Flatware**, $30 to $50 for a 5-piece setting, *from Pottery Barn; 800-922-5507 for catalog.* **Camp stove** *from G&M Sales, 1667 Market Street, San Francisco, CA, 94103; 415-863-2855.*

page 103
Picnic basket *from Basketville, Main Street P.O. Box 710, Putney, VT 05346; 802-387-5509.* Glass **bottle with stopper**, $12, *from Pavilion Antiques, 610 Sir Francis Drake Boulevard, San Anselmo, CA 94960; 415-459-2002.*

page 109
Lemonade jar, $25.74, *from Legacy Antiques, 204 Sir Francis Drake Boulevard, San Anselmo, CA 94960; 415-457-7166.*

POLYNESIAN BASH
Special thanks to the Maui Prince Hotel, Steve Amaral of the Kea Lani Hotel, Gordon Czernick of Makani Gardens, Jack and Julie Kean, and Toby Morris. Special thanks also to Lisa Hammerquist.

pages 112 to 125
Tropical flowers and **leis** *from Cindy's*

Lei Shop, 1034 Maunakea Street, Honolulu, HI 96817; 808-536-6538; and Na Pua O Maui Florist, 1215 South Kihei Road, Kihei, Maui, HI 96753; 800-423-2255 or 808-879-0696.* Custom-made **metal trays** by Klatt Sheet Metal; 516-722-3515. **Specialty ingredients** *from Balducci's, 424 Sixth Avenue, New York, NY 10011; 800-225-3822 or 212-673-2600; and Dean & DeLuca, 560 Broadway, New York, NY 10012; 800-221-7714 or 212-431-1691.* **Sugar-cane products** *from Rimfire Imports, 831 Eha Street, Wailuku, Maui, HI 96793; 808-242-6888. To the trade only.* **Ti leaves** *available through florists.*

page 112
Hawaiian shirts, $30 to $65, *from Bailey's Antiques & Aloha Shirts, 517 Kapahulu Avenue, Honolulu, HI 96815; 808-734-7628.*

page 114
Hula skirts, $14.50 to $18, *from Radio Hula, 169 Mercer Street, New York, NY 10012; 212-226-4467.* **Tiki torches** *available at garden centers, hardware stores, and housewares stores.*

page 115
Bamboo flatware, $155 for a 5-piece setting, *from Takashimaya, 693 Fifth Avenue, New York, NY 10022; 212-350-0100.*

page 119
Handwoven **mats** *from Orchids of Hawaii, 611B Fayette Avenue, Mamaroneck, NY 10543; 800-223-2124 or 914-698-1955.* **Stoneware cups**, $65 for 4, *from William Lipton, Ltd., 27 East 61st Street, New York, NY 10021; 212-751-8131.*

page 121
Votive glasses and **vases** *from Crate & Barrel, 650 Madison Avenue, New York, NY 10022; 800-323-5461 or 212-308-0011.* **Bamboo stakes** *available at garden centers and hardware stores.*

page 123
Straw trivet, $20, *from Craft Caravan, 63 Greene Street, New York, NY 10012; 212-431-6669.*

page 125
littala frosted-glass **salad plate**, $15, *from Ad Hoc Softwares, 410 West Broadway, New York, NY 10012; 212-925-2652.*

BIRTHDAY PARTY

Special thanks to the Miller family. Special thanks also to Sal, Lisa, Laura, and Juliana Salibello; Katie, Jake, and Jilly Horowitz; Henri and Roy Elfassi.

page 126
Pink M&Ms, $8.76 per pound, *from FAO Schweetz at FAO Schwarz, 767 Fifth Avenue, New York, NY 10153; 212-644-9400.* 1"-by-⅞" **scallop-edge labels,** $6 for 24, *from Bell'occhio, 8 Brady Street, San Francisco, CA 94103; 415-864-4048. No catalog.* 3"-by-5" and 8¼"-by-3½" **cellophane bags,** $4 and $7.50 for 100, *from New York Cake & Baking Distributor, 56 West 22nd Street, New York, NY 10010; 800-942-2539 or 212-675-2253.* Sour apple **gummies** and candy **fruit slices,** $3.99 per pound, *from The Sweet Life, 63 Hester Street, New York, NY 10002; 212-598-0092.*

page 127
Hand-pressed **lollipops** by L.C. Good Candy Co., Inc., *from Bourbon Street Candy Stores, 357 Menlo Park Mall, Edison, NJ 08837; 908-494-6255.*

page 128
Pustefix **bubbles,** $2, *from Penny Whistle Toys, 448 Columbus Avenue, New York, NY 10024; 212-873-9090.* **Licorice root,** $3.50 per ¼ pound, *from Aphrodisia, 264 Bleecker Street, New York, NY 10014; 212-989-6440.*

page 129
Oversize **dinner plates,** $6.95 each, *from Fishs Eddy, 889 Broadway, New York, NY 10003; 212-420-9020.* 1850s French **country table,** $6,400, *from Rooms & Gardens, 290 Lafayette Street, New York, NY 10012; 212-431-1297.*

page 137
Mosquito net, $95, *from Portico Bed and Bath, 139 Spring Street, New York, NY 10012; 212-941-7722.* **Assorted ribbons** by Offray *available at sewing stores.* ⅝" to 2" wire-edge **patterned ribbons** *from Hyman Hendler & Sons, 67 West 38th Street, New York, NY 10018; 212-840-8393.* Large green-glass **cake stand,** $65, *from Wolfman-Gold & Good, 117 Mercer Street, New York, NY 10012; 212-431-1888.* 1840s French **iron table,** $3,400, *from Rooms & Gardens, see above.*

PICTURE CREDITS

PHOTOGRAPHY

Melanie Acevedo
pages 68, 69, 70, 71, 72, 73, 74, back cover
(bottom)

Reed Davis
page 86 (top)

Todd Eberle
pages 9, 34, 36, 37, 38, 40, 41, 42, 44, 45,
88, 90, 91, 92, 93, 94, 95, 96, 97, 99, 138,
back cover (third row, right)

Dana Gallagher
page 118

Thibault Jeanson
pages 3, 5, 143

James Merrell
cover, pages 2, 4, 6, 7, 76, 77, 78, 79, 80,
81, 82, 83, 84, 85, 86 (bottom), 87, 126, 127,
128, 129, 130, 132, 133, 134, 135, 137, back
cover (second row, left; third row, left)

Victoria Pearson
pages 8, 10, 11, 12, 13, 14, 15, 16, 17, 18, 21,
22, 24, 25, 26, 28, 29, 30, 32 (right), 33, 46,
48, 49, 50, 51, 52, 53, 55, 56, 57, 58, 59, 60,
61, 62, 63, 64, 65, 66, 67, 100, 101, 102, 103,
104, 105, 106, 108, 109, 110, 112, 114, 115,
116, 117, 119, 120, 121, 122, 123, 125, 142,
back cover (top row, left and right; second
row, right; third row, center)

Maria Robledo
page 32 (left)

ILLUSTRATIONS

Harry Bates
page 50

RECIPE INDEX

*If you have enjoyed this book, please join us
as a subscriber to* MARTHA STEWART LIVING
*magazine. The annual subscription rate is $26
for ten issues. Call toll-free 800-999-6518, or
visit our Web site, www.marthastewart.com.*